This book is written in loving memory of the first Lily in my life, and dedicated to the future of the second.

MR MUSIC MAN
My Life in Showbiz

Mervyn Conn
with
Andrew Crofts

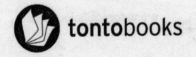

Published in 2010 by Tonto Books Limited
Copyright © Mervyn Conn and Andrew Crofts 2010
All rights reserved
The moral rights of the authors have been asserted

1

ISBN-13:
9781907183188

British Library Cataloguing in Publication Data:
A catalogue record for this book is available from the
British Library

Cover design and photo section by
Elliot Thomson at www.preamptive.com

Printed & bound in Great Britain
by CPI Cox & Wyman

Tonto Books Ltd
Produced up north
United Kingdom

www.tontobooks.co.uk

★ Contents ★

★ Foreword ★

In London in the autumn of 1968, after doing a radio programme for the BBC, I was enjoying a lunch in a pub near Broadcasting House with some BBC people, media 'types' and record company folk when someone mentioned the name Mervyn Conn. There was much laughter and merriment around the table about the dreams this man had for organizing a country music festival at Wembley Arena for the following spring. That got my attention.

'He won't be able to sell enough tickets to fill his own living room,' someone joked.

I made a mental note to look this Mervyn up and find out more about his plans. My chance came when he arrived in Nashville to meet some important folks in the music business. I was much impressed, as were many of these highly respected people who were now helping him to make his dream into a reality.

The first International Festival of Country Music happened the following Easter and was a huge success. Suddenly Mervyn had a lot of new friends and supporters, including some of the guys who had been mocking him in that pub just a few months before.

The following year the BBC was filming the festival and I was asked to host Britain's first country music television series. Thanks to Mervyn and his wild dreams, my whole life had changed. He made country cool for a whole generation of fans in Britain and Europe and he was brave enough to go where no other promoter had gone before. He helped many US country stars make it into the British pop charts and on to the front pages of the national and regional press. He raised the awareness of country music, which helped many more artists to become established. He has done more for the country music scene in Britain than any other person and the whole business owes him a huge debt of gratitude. Without his stubborn genius as a promoter the country boom in the UK in the 1970s and 1980s would never have happened.

George Hamilton IV

★ European ★
★ Roots

Discovering I was going to be a father again at the age of seventy-three was a shock, but then a good life is always full of surprises because most of them make it a more interesting and enriching experience. None of us can ever predict when we start out on life's journey where we are going to end up or what is going to befall us along the way.

The arrival of little Lily two years ago has made me stop and think back over some of the things that have happened to me, or that I have made happen, over the last three quarters of a century and through my own story I can pretty much make out the outline of what has happened in music and entertainment generally.

Born into a time when Al Jolson was the biggest star in the world and Vera Lynn had yet to make her first radio broadcast with the Joe Loss Orchestra, I grew up to be actively involved in the birth of rock and roll, which must rate as one of the most conspicuous cultural changes of the last half century. I have been instrumental in helping many of the world's greatest rock and roll and country stars to make a good living from their music and I have had the good fortune actually to experience the pleasure of hundreds of thousands of people as they enjoyed the shows that I made happen.

Yet, like the vast majority of people, when I set out on my adult life I had no idea in what direction it would take me.

In the early hours of the morning of 5 February 1934, in the Salvation Army's Mothers' Home in Clapton, my mother, Lily Cohen, a woman who pretty much remained the love of my life until the day she died, delivered me into the world. The home had a good reputation in the area and didn't turn anyone away, whatever their religion. As far as I know, the fact that we were obviously a Jewish family was not a problem. In fact, I don't think the question of our religious background even came up. Clapton was a good place to live in those times, a nice middle class area, not like it is today.

On the surface life seemed simpler in those days, perhaps because there was less information available in the pre-television, pre-internet age. In fact, momentous changes were already underway, particularly for families like ours who had their roots deeply entwined in the Jewish diaspora. Sir Oswald Mosley and his Blackshirt fascists were parading around the streets of the East End, spreading their messages of hate, and a few months after my arrival on earth Adolf Hitler declared himself Führer in Germany. Stalin was already instigating his massacres in Russia, but that all seemed a long way from the peaceful streets of pre-war London, seen through the eyes of a small boy resting confidently in the protection of a doting and powerful mother.

The entertainment world was different too, and in Britain the stars were almost exclusively white, even when the songs themselves were of black origin, coming as many of them did from the laments of slaves on the plantations of America and the Caribbean. Al Jolson, the first Jewish superstar, was blacking up to sing shamelessly sentimental songs like 'Swanee' and 'My Mammy'. He was known as the 'world's greatest entertainer', but anyone trying such a blatantly racist act these days would soon find themselves up in court. Although we wouldn't have known it in Britain, things were just starting to change in that area too. In Harlem that year the Apollo Theatre re-opened and would soon become the most famous showcase in the world for genuine black singers and musicians, although it would still be many years before they would be allowed to break through and compete with white acts as equals on every stage and screen.

While crooners like Bing Crosby soothed the nerves of the world, reassuring us that all was well, the forces of law and order were fighting their final battles with gangsters like John Dillinger and Bonnie and Clyde on the streets of America, and Europe was falling deeper and deeper into a political turmoil that would eventually erupt into a war that would result in a new world order a decade later.

My parents were able to protect me from all this and my little world revolved around my family and my home, particularly around Lily, my mother. Dad was a London taxi driver at the time of my arrival, nearly always out of the house trying to make a living driving around the streets of the capital. The world was still reeling from the Great Depression and things were tough for everyone financially. You only survived if you worked every hour you could and were extremely careful with whatever money you were able to scrape together. Luckily we also had older family members who could help my parents get started in the traditional way. My paternal grandfather had bought them a house in Gunton Road and they rented out the upstairs in order to make ends meet and give them a bit more income. Having lodgers didn't bother me because I had never known any different and my mother made me feel totally secure about living in a house full of people.

My father was a scrupulously honest, honourable and sincere man, but he was never a good businessman and didn't enjoy being given too much responsibility. If he had been born fifty years later he would probably have been an intellectual of some sort, maybe tucked safely away in a university somewhere, but in those days such choices would have been an unthinkable luxury for a family like ours. All the men in the community had to concentrate on making enough money to keep everyone fed and secure. By the time I was born, Dad had already tried his hand in the family greengrocery business, where his first job was driving the delivery lorry. Before they bought him the house, my father's parents had given him a shop of his own in Richmond, and it was above that shop that I was conceived. This first business did not do too well and Mum and Dad soon moved to Clapton, to the house in Gunton Road,

3

which I remember as my first home, and Dad had gone on the cabs while he tried to work out what he should do next.

He was an incredibly meticulous man, noticing every detail, not able to tolerate anything out of place around the house. I take after him in that, which is why I was good in showbusiness – I was always paying attention to the details, always wanting to be in control of everything that was going on around me. At home I dare say both he and I were quite tough to live with, wanting complete order and cleanliness around us at all times. I guess now we might be diagnosed as having Obsessive Compulsive Disorder, but whatever it was it served us both well, making us ordered in our thinking and hard working in our drive to make things perfect.

Perhaps it was the desire to create order from the surrounding disorder and uncertainty of those years that characterized our family history. Like most Jewish families in London at the time, we had arrived from a variety of troubled and disrupted backgrounds. My paternal grandmother's family name was Blow and they came from Poland or Austria, depending on where the border was at any given moment. They were from upper-middle-class society and after landing in England they became the first Jewish fruit farmers in Kent, supplying goods to the traders in the markets of Spitalfields and Covent Garden, so elegantly romanticized by George Bernard Shaw in *Pygmalion* and later in the musical adaptation of the play, *My Fair Lady*. Covent Garden actually continued to be a bustling fruit, veg and flower market until the 1970s, when traffic congestion in central London finally made it unsustainable and it underwent a transformation into the equally thriving tourist area that it is today. The Blows were quite well to do by the standards of the time and one of my grandmother's relatives was the famous abstract artist Sandra Blow, who died in 2006.

My paternal grandfather was also an immigrant from Poland and opened a greengrocer's shop in Bow at the very heart of cockney East London. His marriage to my grandmother produced twelve children, of which my father was one of the favourites. I'm told he was indulged by his mother in much the same way I would later be indulged by Lily, which can't have

4

been easy when there were eleven other siblings in need of food and attention, although of course children were forced to become self-sufficient much earlier in those days, the older girls helping their mothers to run the home and look after the small ones, the boys going out to look for work as soon as they were able.

On the other side of my family my maternal grandfather, Jacob Blummenfeld, had arrived in England from southern Russia, where he had run a travelling circus, which perhaps explains how the urge to be showman came to be in my blood. He first met my grandmother in Romania when she was only fifteen years old and immediately decided he wanted to marry her. Her family refused permission (I guess most responsible parents would be nervous about handing their young daughter over to a man who was passing through town with the travelling circus, however romantic the proposal might seem), but my grandfather did not give up, returning with the circus a couple of years later and asking again. His persistence paid off and my grandmother's parents gave their consent to the union. The young couple were married when my grandmother was still only seventeen.

Disappointingly, my grandfather then gave up the circus life and settled in Romania, taking an extremely respectable-sounding job 'licensing rivers'. In the late nineteenth century, however, the anti-Semitic pogroms in the area were making it dangerous to be Jewish and my grandparents decided to travel to England, changing their name to the slightly more anglicized Bloomfield. Things should have gone better for them there, but my grandfather drank a lot, which was unusual for a Jewish man in those days. Who knows what regrets he might have had about leaving behind the excitement and freedom of the circus and the travelling life? The restrictions and responsibilities of family life have weighed down the spirits of many men before and after him. People never discussed their inner thoughts and emotions in those days, especially with children, so my mother never knew the causes of his problem, or if she did, she never passed them on to me. Everyone was too busy simply surviving

5

and making a living to worry about things like feelings. I'm guessing the alcohol probably helped to dull the discomfort of whatever might have been troubling him by the time he arrived in Britain.

In London Grandfather Bloomfield found it hard to get a job and so, like so many other immigrant men, he became a trader, selling clothing in the local markets, living on his wits and physically hauling his stall and stock around the streets to his various pitches. Despite their problems, he and my grandmother eventually had eight children, one of whom was Lily, my mother. As the years passed Grandfather Bloomfield's drinking became more and more of a problem for my grandmother until eventually she decided she'd had enough and left him and their three eldest sons, returning to Romania with the smaller children. Life over there, however, must have been even harder than living with my grandfather, because she soon came back. It seems there was no easy way for anyone to escape life's difficulties in those days. In some ways maybe that was a good thing and kept families together in a way that tends not to happen now.

Although things were better in Britain than in Europe, anti-Semitism was still more of a problem in London in the pre-war years than it is now, partly because we were the most recent immigrants. It seems that the latest people to get off the boats are always the ones others fear most deeply, and consequently hate and despise the most. It was rare to see an African or Asian face in London, so any resentment people might feel towards newcomers was directed towards the Jews. This natural suspicion and hatred was being artificially fuelled by the likes of Oswald Mosley, the British politician and aristocrat who had founded the British Union of Fascists and who entertained Adolf Hitler as a guest at his second wedding. Mosley's fascists soon fell from favour, of course, once the true nature of what was happening in Germany became clearer to the British public, but that didn't change the fact that there were many people who still believed some of the propaganda being disseminated about Jews.

6

Despite this growing public mood, however, my mother's family suffered virtually no trouble, mainly because all five of her brothers were over six feet tall and renowned fighters. In fact, several of them were professional boxers, and my Uncle Jack, who was the most successful of them, became the British European Cruiserweight champion, known to his public as 'Gentleman Jack'. He was the first man to box outdoors at the newly opened Wembley Stadium in 1924 for the eliminator to fight George Carpentier, having knocked out the famous Bombardier Billy Wells. (Uncle Jack was so excited at achieving the knockout that he picked Billy up off the canvas, giving himself a hernia in the process.) He fought a man called Goddard, even though he wasn't completely fit, and was beaten on points after twenty rounds, after which he retired from boxing and headed off to Hollywood. For a while he went into movies (a sort of early version of Vinnie Jones or Arnold Schwarzenegger, I guess), working with stars like Charlie Chaplin, before coming back and opening a famous pub in Leicester Square called The Bear.

It must have been exciting for him to go to America for the first time. I did it myself forty years later when transatlantic flights were commonplace and I know how exciting that was, so I can only imagine what a great adventure it would have been for a young London lad from Jack's background to find himself living and working in the middle of the first 'Golden Age' of Hollywood. Just getting there in the days before long-distance air travel must have been a lifetime's experience in itself.

Wembley, the scene of his great fight, was a venue that I would later get to know very well indeed when my own career took off. Around half a century later, I was the first man to organize country music festivals there, introducing some of the most famous names in America to the European public. Boxing and showbusiness have always been the traditional routes out of the ghettoes.

A Wartime ★
★ Childhood ★

My mother was only twenty-one years old when her mother died, which must have had a considerable effect on her personality. Her father, however, lived to be ninety-nine years old, despite all the alcohol he had imbibed – or maybe because of it, who knows? Not yet married, Mum went to live with her older sister, my Auntie Rae, who had a daughter, Sylvia, and two sons, Mike and Bernie, who were destined to play a large part in my own childhood and many years later, in the early days of television, would become household names all over Britain as the comedy duo Mike and Bernie Winters.

One Saturday night my father went to a dance hall in Islington, no doubt hoping, as most young men do in those situations, that he would meet a nice young girl. Things, however, did not go well for him that night. Being a stranger to the place, he caught the attention of some anti-Semitic local lads, who were doubtless reluctant to share the local talent with someone they viewed as an unwelcome outsider and an interloper on their territory. They were closing in on him and he had probably resigned himself to getting a beating when he spotted an intimidating-looking group of enormous young Jewish men walking over to see what all the trouble was about. As soon as his tormentors saw that he might have some support they immediately melted away and my father found he'd had his first experience of the protective powers of the family that he would eventually marry into.

My mother understood the harsh realities of the world that they lived in just as well as her brothers did. She knew you had to fight and work for every opportunity and that if you did that with enough ferocity and tenacity there was no limit to what you could achieve. Once I was old enough to understand she continually drummed into me the lessons that she felt had stood her and her brothers in good stead. She was determined that I would learn to stand on my own two feet and make a success of whatever I chose to do in life.

She had another baby after me, but he died at seven months, and as far as I know she never tried again, so all her maternal attention, ambition and energy were focused on giving me the best start in life she possibly could. She had high hopes for me from the start and I was always keen to find a way to make her proud. Sometimes I wish my sibling had lived because it would be nice to have someone else to talk to now about our distant past, someone else to share the memories of those early days and of those people who have long since passed away. But at the time I never minded being an only child because there were so many other family members around to keep me entertained and because Mum and I were so close I wouldn't have wanted to share her with a needy little brother or sister. I have always liked being the centre of attention, as reluctant to share the limelight as most other only children.

'You must always do everything you can to be successful in life, Mervyn,' Lily would tell me over and over, inspiring me always to push a little bit harder with anything I might decide to do.

'Always have a pound in your pocket,' was another of her sayings. 'To get on in life you have to have a bit of money behind you.'

She could remember all too well what it felt like to have no money at all, having been through times as a girl when she had to walk to work with cardboard covering the holes in her shoes because she couldn't afford to get them repaired. She was determined to equip me with whatever skills I needed to avoid the poverty trap that caught so many people sooner or later, but at the same time she never tried to persuade me to play safe and get a regular job once I was old enough.

Despite the fact that my parents were often struggling financially and the outside world was preparing for war, I

10

remember the house in Clapton as being a tranquil family oasis under Lily's firm rule. There was a garden out the back that seemed big to me and there were friendly neighbours all around to make me feel safe and protected. The key to the front door hung inside the letterbox on a piece of string so I could let myself in if ever Mum was out at work when I got home from school or playing with a friend. Relatives came and went and Mum and I would go out on shopping trips together. It was a comfortable, comforting pattern of life.

My father, no doubt at my mother's instigation, decided to give up being a taxi driver and to have another go in the greengrocery business, renting premises at the end of our road. He carefully fitted the shop out and was ready to open on 2 September 1939. The following day the Second World War officially broke out and everything changed. I think Dad felt as close to despair at that moment as he ever would. It must have felt as if the whole world was against him in his efforts to improve his family's fortunes.

Like everyone else at the time, my mother was immediately anxious about what was going to happen next, and agonized over what she should do to ensure that I was as safe as possible. All mothers of boys must have been horribly aware of how many millions of young men had died in the previous European conflict, which had ended just twenty years earlier. Rumours were rife that the Germans would be opening hostilities by targeting London and like many parents she thought it wiser to evacuate me out of the city before the bombs started to drop. Along with thousands of other kids I was labelled, equipped with a gas mask and loaded on to a train destined for the market town of Bridgewater in the depths of Somerset. It felt like a grand and rather frightening adventure to be separated for the first time from the family that I had always taken for granted and the mother I adored.

The people I was placed with were a kindly couple with two sons of their own who were a little older than me and had a splendid go-kart, which they would ride at exhilarating speeds down a nearby hill. The first time they put me into the driving seat, however, I was hurled off at speed and hurt my back on landing. Being good, responsible people, the boys' parents informed my mother of the accident. She immediately boarded a train to come to my rescue, sweeping me back to London so that she could take care of my safety herself. Go-karts, it seemed, presented a greater potential danger in her eyes than the Luftwaffe, who had still not appeared in the skies above London.

A strange sort of calm had descended on the city. Everyone was still waiting to see what would happen next. I'd enjoyed a perfectly nice time in Somerset, but I was still glad to be back home again. It was beginning to look as if everyone had been worrying about nothing regarding the intentions of the Germans.

A few months after my return, having been lulled into a false sense of security that nothing too bad was going to befall us, my mother and I were out in a local nursery buying some plants for the garden when we heard the drone of approaching enemy planes for the first time. Suddenly the whole world seemed to be exploding around us. The sky turned red as flames took hold of the surrounding buildings, the earth shaking beneath our feet and the noise blocking out everyone's screams as they ran for cover. Within minutes the peaceful streets of Clapton had turned into a panic-filled nightmare of fire and rubble, fulfilling every parent's worst nightmares.

During the previous months one of our neighbours had been building an Anderson shelter in their garden, which we had been invited to use, but it still wasn't quite finished and Mum decided we would be safer going down into the underground at night. The nearest tube station was Manor House, which we had to get to on the electric trolley bus. Each day over the coming weeks she would pack a little suitcase full of food and set off with me in tow. Auntie Rae was living in Stamford Hill at the time so we would meet her and her children, Mike, Bernie and Sylvia, when we got there.

Being five years older than me, Bernie was the closest in age, and we became closer still during those war years. He and Mike were like the big brothers I never had, although Mike was less interested in bothering with me at that age, wanting to show how grown up he was. I guess Bernie liked having an eager young sidekick and co-conspirator to lead astray, instead of having to be the younger brother all the time. During the long evenings we spent sheltering in the tunnels under north London he and I would ride the trains together while Mum and Auntie Rae and the other grown-ups sorted themselves out with spaces to eat and sleep for the night. We would arrive back at Manor House in time to eat and bed down with the rest of the family on the platform. It must have been awful for the adults but to Bernie and me it just seemed like yet another new adventure.

When the nearby Anderson shelter was finished Mum decided it was safe for us to sleep there and we gave up the trips to Manor House, until the night when a bomb dropped just across the road and she decided it was time to get right out of London until the hostilities were over. By that stage Dad had given up all hope of getting the shop going and was working as an ambulance driver, so he could do his job in any part of the country.

'We're going to move to Oxford,' Mum announced.

I think she must have believed Oxford would be safe from the bombs because it was a university town. We certainly didn't have any family or friends to take us in once we got there, or any clue about how to find somewhere to live. I suppose at a time when refugees were constantly moving from country to country the thought of setting off into an unknown future was less frightening than it might be today. My father's brother, another Uncle Jack, had a car, which was still quite unusual in the East End at that time, and he agreed to drive Mum, me and my cousin Sylvia down there. We had got as far as a town called Headington when the light began to fade and Mum instructed her brother-in-law to stop the car in a shopping street and let us out.

Always optimistic about life, seldom without a smile on her face, Mum had more front than Selfridges. Taking control of the situation as usual, she climbed out and strode into a

13

newsagent called Tillings, Sylvia and me trotting behind her. It looked like the staff were getting ready to close for the night.

'Can I help you?' a kindly looking woman enquired, probably realizing that this businesslike lady was looking for more than a newspaper.

'Do you know of anywhere where the children and I can stay for the night?' Mum asked, getting straight to the point.

Within a few minutes the woman found herself agreeing to let us sleep on the floor of the shop with all our worldly possessions gathered around us, while my uncle drove himself back to London. For some children it might have been a rather alarming experience to find yourself homeless and camping out on the floor of a stranger's shop, but Mum somehow managed to make it seem like an adventure and like she was completely in control of the whole situation, so there was nothing for Sylvia and me to worry about.

Once we had woken up the following day she set about making enquiries around the neighbourhood and found a woman who was willing to take us into her very small house. At least now we had a base and a few days later Mike and Bernie followed us down from London to be with their sister and me. Their dad, Samuel Weinstein, better known to everyone, including his own sons, as 'Mougie', was running a gambling club in Soho's Denman Street and was reluctant to leave the city. The family had all been living in the Regent Palace Hotel near Piccadilly Circus, which had once been the biggest hotel in Europe with over a thousand rooms, and which stood right at the heart of London's West End. Although they must have felt pretty safe in such a huge, solid building, the air raids were intensifying, and when Uncle Jack's pub in Leicester Square was hit by a bomb Uncle Mougie realized he was going to have to take some decisions regarding the safety of his boys. Luckily for Uncle Jack the raid happened after closing time when he was already walking away from the pub across Leicester Square, so he was safe, but his faithful old barman was killed and the building was completely destroyed. When another bomb hit an annex of the hotel Uncle Mougie could no

14

longer delay and it was decided that London was becoming too dangerous for Mike and Bernie to stay up in town any longer.

I was delighted to have my two heroes with me again and almost immediately upon their arrival Bernie and I set about digging up our hostess's lovely garden, which didn't go down well. But she must have taken to us, because she didn't chuck us out, and we were enrolled at the local school in Headington so that our education could continue.

The war disrupted and affected everyone's lives, taking us all to places we would otherwise never have dreamed of going to, and causing any number of unlikely meetings and alliances. My Uncle Jack, the one who had driven us down to the country, joined the Eighth Army and met my mother's younger brother, Uncle Connie, in the desert campaign in Tunisia. Many years later, when I eventually married, I discovered that my father-in-law was a captain in the same campaign. At the time I had no idea that all these connections were happening in the adult world that seemed so distant from my own life of childhood adventures.

Although we were no longer in London, we still stayed in touch with a number of other members of the family. My mother's brother, Mick, was stationed down at Dover in the artillery and he used to come down and visit us from time to time. He was another impressive figure, being well over six foot tall, and I grew almost as close to him in those formative years as Mum was, laying the foundations of a relationship that would last for many years.

It wasn't long before Mum decided we needed more space and found us half a house to rent in Cowley, which was owned by a lovely woman called Mrs Kitchener. At this point Dad came down from London to join us, as well as Auntie Netta and her baby son, Adrian. Dad had been injured in a bombing raid and was not able to drive his ambulance for a while. Once he arrived in Oxford, however, he became attached to the RAF and when he was fit again he was given a sixty-foot-long articulated lorry to drive around the country, picking up crashed planes. Most of them were German bombers which had

15

been shot down and which still contained the mangled and burned bodies of their crews. Being a sensitive man, Dad found the work deeply traumatizing, and I'm not sure he ever managed to shake the images of the scenes he saw during those years from his head. He used to bring souvenirs back for Bernie and me, like German crosses and bits of Perspex that we could make rings from.

I was given a little black mongrel of my own, called Blackie, who I took with me everywhere and I think the following years may have been the happiest and most carefree of my life. Away from the dangers of the city Bernie and I were allowed to go wherever we pleased whenever we were out of school, as long as we stayed out of trouble. We spent hours wandering around the countryside with Blackie, blackberrying, swimming and punting on the river, lost in our own imaginary world, completely unconcerned about whatever was happening elsewhere, confident that the adults in the family were taking care of everything on our behalves.

Even though we were miles from the West End of London, the magical lure of showbusiness and entertainment still managed to reach us thanks to the radio and cinema. I remember how the whole family used to sit around together listening to the radio in the evenings – the adventures of *Dick Barton – Special Agent* and the *It's That Man Again* comedies were my particular favourites, allowing me to escape into other worlds and imagine what it might feel like to make audiences laugh and applaud.

Once a week we'd put on a little show for the grown-ups with Bernie doing impressions and me singing a song, imagining I was Al Jolson, while Mum and the others cheered wildly. Mike had a clarinet, which he was very serious about. He and Bernie were already starting to think about being professional entertainers and used to disappear off to perform for the Canadian servicemen billeted in the area, which annoyed me because it meant that I got left behind. I also used to get left behind when Bernie managed to talk his way into the local dances. He was only about twelve years old but he was always a big lad, which I definitely wasn't, so I had to wait outside for

16

him, which was really frustrating and made me long all the more to be like him.

The government and the local community did all they could to help evacuees. The council put on cartoon shows in the local cinema for us and school milk was free, but there were no free lunches, and Mum would make us sandwiches each day, or I would walk home for food. Things like sweets were virtually unheard of until the American servicemen started to come over and my cousin Sylvia became an object of interest to them. She would invite these seemingly glamorous and wealthy creatures to the house for parties, which meant Bernie and I could get chewing gum and Hershey bars. Sylvia actually met her future husband while we lived in the country. He worked as barber down in the town. She would bring him home and I would make a point of sitting with them until they gave me a shilling to go to bed and allow them some time alone – just like that Billy J Kramer hit of the sixties, 'Little Children'.

I also developed my first taste for card games during those years. My mother used to play poker with friends, most often upstairs at the local hairdressers. I would watch, fascinated, as the women gambled tiny amounts of money, which seemed like fortunes to me at the time. She also used to play a game called Kaluki, which is a kind of Rummy, with a friend called Coxy, a nice man who used to be able to get a bit of fish for us now and then.

As well as running a club in Soho, Mike and Bernie's dad – Uncle Mougie – was a professional gambler, making his living at racetracks or by just hustling strangers on trains or anywhere else where he could persuade them to start up a game. He had taught his sons all the games, which they then taught me. We passed endless hours competing and exercising our brains in this way. Dad used to play solo, so he taught me the rules to that game as well, adding to my repertoire.

We had absolutely no money during those years, but we didn't need any because rationing was on so there was virtually nothing to buy anyway. I do remember, though, walking past a greengrocer's with Mum one day and seeing a box of golden-pink fruits that I had never seen before, which they were selling

17

for two shillings each (ten pence in today's money, which was a lot then).

'What are they?' I asked.

'They're peaches,' she replied.

'Can we buy one?'

'For two shilling!' she exclaimed, looking at me as if I was from another planet. 'Are you mad?'

It was impossible for Bernie and me to stay out of trouble for long, like the time when we destroyed a haystack after deciding to build a camp inside it. The farmer caught us in the act, furiously waving a shotgun at us.

'A few years ago I would have shot you two,' he told us. 'Instead you can leave your bikes here with me until you come back with half a crown to pay for me to get this re-stacked.'

Walking all the way home and having to ask Mum for half a crown was a hard lesson, but we had no choice: we needed our bikes to fully enjoy our freedom and the grown-ups would very soon have noticed if they had disappeared, which would mean answering a lot of very awkward questions.

Another day Bernie and I walked all the way down to Oxford and on the way back we came across a dump full of old cars and other scrap – heaven for two young boys. Rummaging around, we found a loose car seat and decided it would be useful and carried it for miles to get it home. When we got there we found Dad waiting on the doorstep for us with folded arms.

'Where did you get that from?' he demanded as we came staggering in with the seat. 'You've stolen it, haven't you?'

It hadn't felt like stealing at the time because it seemed it had been deliberately abandoned, but now he had put it like that I began to get doubts. I said nothing; just stared at the floor and waited to see what happened next.

'You,' he said to Bernie, 'take it all the way back to where you found it. And you' … he pointed to me … 'are going to get the strap.'

It was the only time I ever remember him beating me, and it was a lesson well learned.

Mum was never quite as scrupulous about honesty as Dad was, taking a more pragmatic approach to whatever she felt had to be done. She used to take us down to the cinema, for instance, and buy a ticket for one of us. Whoever had the ticket would then hold open the back door so the rest of us could get in for free. Dad would definitely not have approved if he had found out, but none of us were going to tell him.

I had been pretty well sheltered from anti-Semitism in England at that time, but Mum had still taught me how to box, just like all my uncles, in case I ever had to defend myself against bigotry. My family name was still Cohen in those days (and Mike and Bernie's was Weinstein), so it was obvious to most people what our religion was. I also made friends with a lad called Stanley Levy. When we moved up to the junior school at the age of seven or eight Stanley and I went to prayers with everyone else every day, just as we had when we were at nursery. About three weeks into our first term, however, the headmaster called us into his office.

'You two boys are Jews,' he announced, 'so you are not to go into prayers any more.'

I couldn't understand why that should be, but I wasn't going to argue with such a senior authority figure. Instead of giving us anything else to do when the others went into assembly, however, he made us sit outside the doors, where the rest of the school would walk past us and see that we had been transformed into outsiders. Those mornings are still fresh in my memory nearly seventy years later, as clear and as humiliating as they were at the time. I felt I had been marked out as different and I got into a fight virtually every day after that for the next few weeks. Thanks to Mum's foresight, of course, I was able to put into practice all the family boxing skills. I refused to be bullied by anyone, throwing myself at any boy who even tried to put me down or pick on me, however big he might be. It didn't take me long to gain a reputation for being fearless and ferocious, despite my size. I also sat next to a big lad called Roy in class, who was an even better fighter than me. We were always together and after a few weeks people learned to steer clear of us. Poor old Stanley Levy, however, wasn't so lucky, and I used to have to escort him home each afternoon to avoid him getting a nasty kicking.

Mike tells a story about a woman he visited at that time who told him in all seriousness that she could always spot Jews 'by the horns growing out of their heads'. Another time a girl he was going out with told him he couldn't be Jewish.

'Why not?' he asked, surprised.

'Because you don't wear the robes,' she replied.

It's not hard to understand how the fascists managed to brainwash so many people into hating the Jews when ignorance was still so widespread, even amongst otherwise well-meaning people.

★ Post–War ★ Youth

On 6 June 1944, when I was ten years old, hundreds of planes flew over us in Oxford, carrying the paratroops to France for D-Day. It was an incredible sight and really exciting for a young boy with an imagination as we all stood in the garden staring up at them droning past. The reality of what was actually happening, however, only came home to me when I heard that a cousin of my father's, Jack, had been killed in the attack.

Although there was still a year before the war would finally be over, to the grown-ups this seemed to signal a turning point, giving them hope that things would be getting back to normal eventually. By then I could barely remember what peacetime had felt like. To me it seemed like there had always been rationing and soldiers in uniforms and serious, posh BBC voices coming out of the radio with news about battles in places with foreign-sounding names.

Once Mum felt it was definitely safe and that there were going to be no more bombing raids we headed back to London to re-start the lives that had been so rudely interrupted. Our original house had been sold and we lived for a while with one of my aunts until Mum and Dad found a flat for us in Lorraine Mansions, Holloway Road and I was enrolled in a school just round the corner from where the new Arsenal Emirates stadium now stands.

I have been an avid Arsenal fan all my life. I could get into the games in their old stadium in Highbury through the schoolboys' entrance for sixpence and got to see legends like Jimmy Logan, Alex Forbes and George Swindon on the pitch.

Ken Fryer, who later became the managing director and a good friend, was the office boy in the days when I first started going to watch matches. I even saw the legendary Denis and Leslie Compton play.

There was never any trouble in the crowds in those days and hardly any bad language to be heard, either on the pitch or off it. It seems to me when I think back that those were kinder, gentler days, when people had more time and consideration for one another. This was the period when the National Health Service and the welfare state were founded and there was a great sense of optimism as to what the future might hold for all of us. It seems like a golden period now, looking back from the chaos of today, and full of hope that things would soon be getting better.

My father went to work as a private hire driver for a while and then returned to the black cabs, still one of the most distinctive features of London street life, along with red double-decker buses, phone boxes and policemen in helmets. Life as a cabbie suited him because he still hated all sort of pressure and responsibility, particularly those inevitably connected with running a shop. He just wanted a quiet, simple life. Luckily for him, however, or maybe unluckily, my mother possessed enough ambition for both of them, which sometimes drove him to distraction.

It wasn't long before Lily had persuaded him to have another go at starting a business and to buy another greengrocer's shop in the St Paul's Road, Highbury. The shop was going to cost £500, which was a lot of money in 1946, more than they would ever have been able to save up out of Dad's income as a cabbie. They were going to have to borrow it. Ordinary people like us never thought to go to banks for loans in those days: in fact, I don't think my parents even had a bank account. If you wanted to borrow money you had to think of someone you knew who may have a little spare and would be willing to trust you enough to lend it. In most cases, this would mean going to a relative.

Dad's brother Jack worked for his father-in-law in a successful fish and chip shop in Camden Town and Uncle Jack said he thought he would be open to investing in a new shop. One of the customers who came to the shop was the movie star Ray Milland, who won the best actor Oscar in 1946 for Billy Wilder's *The Lost Weekend* and apparently used to flirt outrageously with my Aunt Nettie when she was behind the fryer. So Mum persuaded Dad to go to see Uncle Jack's father-in-law and the old man agreed to lend them the money they needed. To keep our outgoings to the absolute minimum until the business was up and running and earning a profit, we moved into the accommodation above the shop.

This time Dad had got it right. The timing, location and all his previous experience came together and the business did well. Food was still scarce in Britain after the shortages of the war and shopkeepers had first access to exotic products like bananas and oranges when they started to come back on to the market. Within a short time the shop was giving us a lifestyle Dad was perfectly happy with, but Mum, who was always looking to the future, went out one day and found other premises to take on, with a view to expanding the business now that it was doing well. It was a perfectly reasonable thing for any business person to do, but when Dad found out he went ballistic. He just didn't want any more debts or financial worries.

They were such different characters I wonder sometimes if their marriage would have lasted so long if they had been born later. In those days, however, couples like my parents stayed together, however uncomfortable that might sometimes have been for them both, partly because no one could afford to divorce and partly because there was still a social stigma attached to failed marriages. When I was older Mum confided in me that the love of her life had actually been a man called Dave Sharpe. Dave came from an upper-class Jewish family who didn't approve of her as a potential daughter-in-law because of her poor family background, so all hopes of her ever marrying him were quickly crushed. Heartbroken but undeterred, Mum looked around for someone else with whom to

23

settle down and start a family. She had a friend called Phoebe whose brother was a friend of Dad's. An introduction was arranged between Lily and Phil, my father, and Mum went to visit his family, where she soon realized that Dad was one of his mother's favourites.

'You really don't think my brother will ever marry you, do you?' one of his sisters said to her when Dad was out of earshot.

'Why not?' Mum asked.

'Because he just won't.'

I think Mum decided at that moment to prove her future sister-in-law wrong. She did not intend to be rejected twice and several months later Lil and Phil got married at the Regent Palace Hotel, once a splendid building originally owned and operated by the J Lyons Corporation, who introduced the famous Lyons Corner Houses to London. The next day the pair were back at work in Dad's first shop in Richmond. Lily told me she never got over her love for the unobtainable Dave Sharpe but in the end she and Dad were together for sixty years, despite their increasingly frequent clashes, and they gave me a wonderful childhood and stable base on which to build my life, so they must have been doing something right.

My father liked to have his life neat and under control. As I said, he was the most meticulously tidy and organized man I have ever met, apart from myself. As a small boy I would always find my toothbrush waiting for me in the bathroom each morning with the toothpaste neatly squeezed out already. There was no excuse for me to skip the first chore of the day, which he viewed as essential. We had no plumbed-in bathtub in our accommodation after our return to London, just a tin one that hung on the wall and had to be put in front of the fire and filled from the kettle if you wanted to use it. Once a fortnight, however, I would be taken to a smart flat near Russell Square, which was owned by another of my father's brothers, and which had a proper modern bathroom. There I would be allowed to have a long, luxurious, hot soak. I would imagine that it was seeing places like that, with simple conveniences that seemed like luxuries to us, that made my mother impatient for us to move up the prosperity ladder a little faster than we were doing.

Wanting me to have a Jewish education, my parents sent me to a Jewish grammar school called Avigdor in Clissold Park when I was eleven years old. Clissold, a beautiful old park in Hackney, was quite a way from Highbury Corner, where we lived, and the daily school trip involved two buses each way. Although there were advantages to being in a school where I was no longer an outsider, no longer part of a minority, I wasn't that keen on my new surroundings. There was a lot of praying and ritual during the course of the school day, which seemed a bit much to me. Although we were a practising Jewish family, none of us made a big fuss about it. We didn't have the time. The school taught us ancient and modern Hebrew as well as all the usual foreign languages.

A lot of boys there had been in the German extermination camps. They had numbers tattooed on their arms and pictures burned into their memories that the rest of us couldn't even imagine. Many of them had lost their parents in those camps and some had lost their whole families. I had seen some of the newsreels about these places, which had been showing in the cinemas, and I was beginning, along with the rest of the world, to understand just how bad it had all been and just how important the outcome of the war had been for Jewish people everywhere.

Blackie, my dog, had come back to London with us but obviously I couldn't take him to school with me, so he would go out during the day with the driver who delivered for my father. But the driver drove off without him one day and by the time he realized his mistake and went back to look for him, Blackie had disappeared. When I got home from school Mum and I went to the spot where the driver thought he had left him, hoping he would still be wandering around searching for us, but there was still no sign. I was heartbroken, but I like to think that someone kind found him and took him in.

In 1947 I went to stay with another of my aunts for a couple of months in Brussels, where she and my uncle ran a restaurant at the heart of the red light district. It was the first time that I had been somewhere where there were no food shortages. The Americans were paying Belgium a lot of money at the time for their uranium in the Belgian Congo and the country seemed incredibly prosperous to me after all the shortages of my childhood in England. For the first time ever I got to taste Coca Cola and I was able to buy sweets whenever I had the money. Even though I was still only twelve years old I would go on day trips by myself while my uncle and aunt worked in the restaurant and I felt very comfortable with the European way of life. I was starting to get a taste for the freedoms of the grown-up world and was eager to leave school and get started on whatever my life's journey was going to turn out to be. My mother seemed to be convinced that whatever I chose to do would turn out to be an enormous success and her total confidence rubbed off on me.

After the war Mum's brother Uncle Mick had gone to live with Mike and Bernie's parents and worked for a man called Wally, who ran a very successful tobacconist shop in Leicester Square. Uncle Mick already knew the West End well because he used to work with Uncle Jack in his pub, before it was bombed out. Wally the tobacconist was a professional gambler, like Uncle Mougie, and Uncle Mick would accompany him to the dogs as his minder.

When Mick married a woman called Iris, he went back into the pub business, opening up premises just round the corner from the Regent Palace Hotel, off Piccadilly Circus. He then moved to Brighton and opened another pub called The Botega for Charlie Forte, who was opening the first outlets in what would eventually become the giant Forte Hotel and Catering Group, one of the most successful and high-profile businesses in post-war England. Iris's sister was married to Max Bygraves's brother, giving the family yet another showbusiness connection. Max, who came from the docklands of London and whose father had been another professional boxer, was already

26

becoming a big star in variety by then. Mick and Iris had a daughter called Mandy, who now lives in the south of France where she runs a beach restaurant with her husband, Rick.

When Uncle Mick's marriage fell apart he came to live with my parents, which was great for my mother because they were so close, but maybe not so great for my Dad. The two men were a bit like Walter Matthau and Jack Lemmon in *The Odd Couple*, always arguing about something. Thinking back now, I guess Dad must have felt a bit left out because of the obvious bond between Lily and Mick.

My father had another brother who was married to Mum's friend, Phoebe (the friend who introduced Mum and Dad). Their two children, Helen and Harvey, were almost as close to me as Mike and Bernie had been, and their family gave me a glimpse of what it was like to have a little bit more money. They had a lovely house in Finchley and used to put up a Christmas tree each year, which Dad never allowed us to do. My whole family was a web of interconnections and shared relationships, which I think helped to make me feel very secure as I prepared myself to go out into the world and make a living.

I was already starting to show signs of being a very practical little businessman. I didn't like doing my homework so I would help Dad out in the shop after school instead. Next door was a sweet shop and I would take fruit to the woman who owned it and she would give me sweets in exchange, which I would take in to school the following day and sell to my sugar-starved schoolmates. My mother's words of advice were always echoing in my mind. Where Dad found her philosophies intimidating, I found them exciting and full of promise. I could see exactly what she was getting at.

'You'll get nothing by working for other people, son,' she'd tell me. 'You've got to work for yourself and be the one telling other people what to do.'

From College to the Kaye Sisters

Despite the distractions of my various out-of-school money-making activities, Mum managed to persuade me to stay in education until I was seventeen. When I did finally leave it was with good enough exam grades to get into Regent Street Polytechnic for a three-year course studying pattern cutting and tailoring, learning how to design, pattern cut and sew, making suits and trousers and everything else that the public might want to wear. It was without doubt a sensible thing to do because at the end of the course I would have my City and Guilds qualification and I would be a trained tailor. Like most sensible parents, Mum and Dad believed it would be a good idea for me to have a skill to fall back on, and maybe I would even become a famous designer. Having lived through the Depression they knew how important it was to have other abilities in hard times and there were plenty of examples of people we had heard of who had made fortunes in the clothing business.

Although I had no overwhelming desire to be a tailor, going to a polytechnic brought another advantage, as it meant I could defer the moment when I would have to go off and do National Service in the army. The Korean War was going on at that time (the one that eventually spawned the successful film and television series *MASH*) and Britain was still dealing with the communists in Malaya and the Mau Mau in Kenya, so there was a real possibility that boys who did National Service would end up facing considerable danger. None of these conflicts seemed to be worth laying your life on the line for and both Lily and I were very keen for me not to get killed before I had even got started on life. National Service formally ended on the last day of 1960, just as the 'swinging sixties' were about to take off, and I managed to avoid ever having to sign up for the army.

The family grocery business was continuing to thrive as the country gradually recovered from the war, goods became more available and people were able to spend more money, although we were still a long way from the prosperous consumer society we enjoy today. We were able to install a proper plumbed-in bath and even bought one of the earliest televisions in 1948, which seemed like the most fantastic thing to me as I watched shows like *Muffin the Mule*, a programme that would look like something from the Stone Age to children now.

So much of the life that I took for granted as a teenager would seem alien to the young of today, like our Sunday evening family rituals. Virtually all shops would be closed on Sundays, and so on Sunday evenings we would all dress up and go down to the West End for a restaurant meal. Even though rationing meant that no one was allowed to spend more than five shillings on any meal, for fear of using more than their fair share of scarce national food resources, we used to make an event of every meal out. It wasn't like now when many families think nothing of popping out for Italian, Indian or Chinese meals several times a week. Everyone would dress up smartly to go into town, the men in suits and ties whatever their backgrounds, the women in dresses and high heels. Our routine was always the same: every week we would go to the Trocadero in Piccadilly Circus, not far from the Regent Palace Hotel, where they had live music playing while we ate. It all seemed wonderfully glamorous and sophisticated to a young boy and the night time streets of Soho seemed full of promise and excitement.

Despite the fact that I was training to be a tailor, I was already totally in thrall to showbusiness, particularly my hero Al Jolson. His life had been made into a movie at the end of the 1940s, starring Larry Parks as Jolson, but the real man's singing voice was dubbed over the soundtrack. He was called the greatest entertainer in the world for many years and I longed to see him perform live. Sadly, he never came to England, which was not unusual for American stars at the time, but I had collected all his records and I dreamed of one day inhabiting the same sort of world as him, the Hollywood-style world I had seen depicted in the movie, without having any idea how I might achieve such an ambitious goal or whether the film was even close to giving a realistic picture of life at the top of the showbusiness tree.

At the same time as attending college I was still working in the family shop, and also making clothes for anyone I could, particularly if they had anything to do with showbusiness and might allow me to glimpse behind the scenes. My cousins Mike and Bernie had changed their name from Weinstein to Winters by then and had gone on to the stage to make their way as professional comics. Mike had gone serious for a while after the war, attending a college in Oxford and the Royal Academy of Music, while Bernie had been playing the ukulele in the Regency Club in Soho, which one of our uncles had an interest in, and doing a bit of stand-up comedy. They were now working as a double act and it seemed to me that they were my potential passport to the life I longed to lead. I would go around with them in the evenings after college, mixing with show people in the nightclubs, particularly the Stork Club in Swallow Street, just off Piccadilly. The club was famous for the hostesses who were hired to entertain businessmen during the week, but on Sunday nights they would have a cabaret night and that was when we wanted to be there. We never had any money, so the three of us would sit at the back, nursing one coffee all evening, while Mike and Bernie would try to persuade the management to let them go on stage. It was there that I first saw Tommy Steele performing, right at the beginning of his career.

Tommy was a cockney lad like us, a couple of years younger than me, and he has often been called the first 'teen idol' or 'rock star', although we wouldn't have known that at the time. People also called him 'the English Elvis' and

31

recently it was accidentally revealed on the radio by the theatre impresario Bill Kenwright that Elvis once made a secret visit to England to meet up with Tommy, who showed him the sights of London. It was the only time Elvis ever set foot in the UK and Tommy had kept the secret for fifty or more years, until Bill let it slip.

While I was meeting as many actors and singers as I could, I got particularly friendly with Stubby Kaye, the American comic actor who was starring in *Guys and Dolls* at the Coliseum. I would make waistcoats for him and the other performers in the production and for some reason Stubby warmed to me and started taking me around London with him as a friend. He even took me to a reception at the American ambassador's residence in Regent's Park and introduced me to people like Sammy Davis Jr, who had started out singing and dancing in vaudeville at the age of three with his father and uncle as part of the Will Mastin Trio and went on to be part of Sinatra's infamous Las Vegas 'Rat Pack'. I was completely knocked off my feet by the whole experience. Along with Mike and Bernie, Stubby was making me even more certain that I wanted to be part of the world of showbusiness. I really wanted to be a professional singer, but at the same time there seemed to be so many other sides to the business that were equally interesting and attractive. But I still couldn't work out how I was going to achieve my goal. I particularly loved all the American crooners like Frank Sinatra and Tony Bennett. The British singers all seemed a bit conservative to me by comparison, until the rock and roll era arrived.

When I left the college with my City and Guilds certificate my first thought was to get a regular income and I initially went to work for a ladies' fashion house called Le Chasse in Mayfair's Hill Street, earning fifteen shillings a week. As in so much of the fashion world the atmosphere was incredibly camp, which didn't bother me, but was very different from the rough, macho world of fighting and gambling that the men in my family usually inhabited. Although I could see that Le Chasse was a good place to work, my mother's words about 'not working for other people if you want to get on' were always at the back of my mind, and the contrast between life on the shop floor during the day and life amongst the theatres and clubs at night was very stark.

It was nice to have a regular wage coming in, of course, but even at that young age I could tell this was no more than a basic living and would never lead to the sort of independence that Lily had always encouraged me to aim for. If I wanted to afford any of the good things in life, and if I wanted to be able to call my time my own, I was going to have to find ways to make money for myself. No one else was going to give it to me.

Like my grandfather, and like many thousands of other entrepreneurs both before and after me, I decided to start supplementing my wages with a market stall of my own. So on the weekends, when I wasn't at Le Chasse, I was working in the local markets of East London like Petticoat Lane, selling clothing I bought from wholesalers, sometimes earning as much as £10 or £12 profit in a single day. I had soon made enough to buy myself a 1938 Morris 10, which I would use to drive myself to and from work in Mayfair. I was aware that I was probably earning more in a day in the markets than the manager of Le Chasse was earning in a week and that I needed to think seriously about finding a better way to employ my time than spending most of my week in the shop. I just needed to come up with the right idea.

Every Saturday night I would go out dancing and chatting up girls with Mike and Bernie and other friends to venues like the Hammersmith Palais, the Lyceum, the Finsbury Park Astoria or the Tottenham Royal, and one night while we were out on the town I bumped into a friend of mine, Bernie Kaye, who was working for a clothing manufacturing company. As we got talking, an idea occurred to me.

'Why don't we start a fashion business together?' I suggested. 'I can design the stuff and you can manufacture it.'

It seemed to me that the area to get into was men's high fashion clothes because I could see that there wasn't anyone

33

else doing that at that time, whereas women's fashion was already well catered for. This was before places like Carnaby Street or the King's Road had become full of boutiques. Most men were still having to wear the same dull outfits as their fathers and their grandfathers before them because there was nothing else in the shops for them to buy. But young men like us were starting to have a bit of money in our pockets and we wanted to cut more of a dash, we wanted to be a bit individual, if only we could find something different to buy. I was sure it could work. Bernie didn't seem averse to the plan so I just had to work out the financial logistics of how we could do it with as little outlay as possible. I handed in my notice at Le Chasse and went to see my father, explaining my plan and asking if I could have access to some of my bar mitzvah money, about £500, which was sitting in a Post Office account, in order to buy a sewing machine. By that time he and Mum had bought us a flat round the corner from the shop, which meant the rooms above the shop, where we had been living before, were standing empty, which gave me another idea.

'Can I use the room above the shop as a workshop?' I asked, and he agreed.

So, Bernie Kaye and I were now in business, and I decided to change my name from Cohen to Conn in order to be a bit more unusual and not sound quite so Jewish. Thinking back, I'm not sure if I ever changed it officially, even though I have now gone by the name of Conn for well over half a century. I'm not certain that it was the best choice. I probably should have gone for something like Collins, but would that have been as memorable as Conn? There's no way of knowing now, the decision was made, and for better or worse 'Mervyn Conn' had been born.

Bernie and I decided to start by making sweaters in hound-stooth check and plain gabardine, edging them in wool to make them a bit different. Although it sounds pretty tame now, there was nothing else like it around at the time. I headed off to John Lewis to buy the material and we put together some samples so that I would have something to sell with. I needed someone to make the wool edging and I unearthed a guy with a knitwear factory in Dalston. He charged me a lot of money, but I was happy with the result. Once the samples were ready I got all dressed up and set off in my Morris 10 with my new order book, feeling optimistic. My first stop was in Holborn and the shop owner liked the look of the samples. He ordered four dozen sweaters.

'When's the delivery?' he asked as I took down his details, unable to believe how easy this was proving to be.

'About four weeks,' I replied, plucking the figure out of the air, not even knowing if I was going to be able to get the amount of material I would need for such a big order but not wanting to say anything that might kill the sale.

'Okay,' he said, signing off on the deal without asking any more questions.

Buoyed with this success, my next stop was Cecil Gee in Charing Cross Road, which was the top shop for men's fashion at that time, soon to become a famous nationwide chain. Cecil himself happened to be in there at the moment I showed up so I laid out the samples for him and went into my sales spiel.

'I like this,' he said almost immediately. 'I'll give you a big order, but I must have exclusive rights in this area.'

I was happy to go along with that – to be honest I would probably have agreed to anything he had asked for at that stage – and he gave me an order for fourteen dozen sweaters across all the sizes and styles. Now I was well and truly on a roll and by the end of the day I had orders for about twenty-two dozen jumpers with no idea how to begin producing them in time for the delivery dates that I had promised. I didn't even know where to go to buy the material I needed. I doubted if John Lewis would have enough in stock.

Bernie's father was a stock cutter for a big manufacturer so we went to him for advice. He sent us to a wholesaler in Soho's Berwick Street. We also needed a special machine to cut several patterns out at one time, otherwise we would never get them done. The wool trim was the next problem. I went back to the guy I had been to before for the samples and the quantities I was now asking for obviously piqued his interest. He became very friendly.

'Show me what you're doing with this wool trim,' he said.

Not knowing any better, I proudly showed him the jumpers, and of course he nicked the idea after giving me my first order. Lesson learned: always play your cards close to your chest for as long as you can.

Confident that we were now on to a good thing, Bernie and I started to plan how to invest in the business and expand it. Caught up in the excitement of making a bit of money and rushing around trying to make everything work, I forgot about my showbusiness ambitions for a while. Mum was as excited by my sudden success as I was and wanted to be involved. Having bought myself a better car, a Riley, I drove up to Leicester with her and we bought two knitting machines so we could produce the trim ourselves. I then had to hire an expert, who also came from Leicester, and put him into digs down in London. My overheads were beginning to rise but it didn't matter because we had the orders to cover them. I had gone in one leap from being a student to being an employer.

I could no longer fit the whole operation into the room above the shop, so I expanded into the basement. But Dad, being such a meticulous and orderly man, was starting to get fed up with all the people and machinery coming and going through his premises while he tried to serve his customers and lay his stock out neatly. He finally decided he'd had enough and gave up the shop, taking another premises in Twickenham, which was miles away. It was a good position, but he and Mum then had to spend a large part of their time each day travelling. They never seemed to mind making sacrifices like that for me. In fact, they seemed to enjoy it.

Business was booming but once I had got things up and running and the novelty of having some money in my pocket had worn off I realized my heart wasn't really in it. Mike and Bernie's act was starting to take off too and it was their sort of world and the theatres and clubs of the West End that I really enjoyed being part of. I was also becoming increasingly keen on women, who I knew were more plentiful around the fringes of the clubs and theatres of the West End than the fringes of garment manufacturing in the East End.

One evening, when Mike, Bernie and I were in the Astor Club, which was in Berkeley Square at the time, behind the Colony Club, I met a girl called Sheila, who was one of the Kaye Sisters, a singing trio who were enormously successful at the time. They had been set up to rival the even more successful Beverley Sisters, who were famous for hits like 'I Saw Mommy Kissing Santa Claus' and 'Little Drummer Boy'.

Unlike the Beverleys, who ended up in the *Guinness Book of Records* in 2002 for being the longest surviving vocal group without a change of lineup, the Kaye Sisters weren't actually sisters in real life. In fact the three of them came from completely different parts of the country. They had taken the name from their manager, Carmen Kaye, and they always wore the same outfits on stage with the same blonde, fringed hairstyles in order to give the impression of a strong family likeness. They used to headline at places like Churchill's and the Colony and had hits with titles like 'Paper Roses', 'Gotta Have Something in the Bank, Frank' and 'Are you Ready, Freddy?' Two of their biggest hits were with Frankie Vaughan, who was a huge star at the time. They had appeared on the Royal Variety Show, which was a major measure of success for anyone in showbusiness, sharing the bill with Judy Garland. They had also broken through in America, following the Beverleys again, who were the first British female group to enter the American charts. The Kayes were invited on to *The Ed Sullivan Show*, which was the biggest variety show of the time and would later introduce both Elvis and The Beatles to the mainstream middle-American audience. Although the traditional vaudeville shows were already dead by that time, *The Ed Sullivan Show* kept to much the same format for many years. Whatever way you looked at it, the Kaye Sisters were right at the top of their game.

I was immediately attracted by Sheila and we started going out together. I couldn't believe my luck. I wasn't much more than a kid and I was actually dating a big star. The experience made me all the more convinced that showbusiness was where my heart lay, even though I was very successful with the clothes and was much more likely to make a fortune there than in the precarious world of entertainment. After a few months, however, I realized I had made a mistake. I was going out with the wrong Kaye sister! I had now fallen for Shan and had to switch my affections, which nearly broke up the act for a short while before things settled down. Imagine the media frenzy there would be now if one man went out with two different members of the Spice Girls or Girls Aloud!

Acts like the Kayes and the Beverleys, however, were about to be replaced in the music charts by something completely new, something that we had already seen hints of with Tommy Steele. The real clue to what was about to happen was to be heard in the voice of Elvis. Everything was about to change.

Rock and roll initially arrived on these shores when Bill Haley and the Comets sang 'Rock Around the Clock', a record which eventually sold about twenty-five million copies, and I was completely sold on the whole idea. I designed an embroidered 'rock and roll jacket' with a guitar on the back, which was an even bigger success for the business than the sweaters had been.

'We've got to expand,' Bernie said, looking around at the bustling chaos that now filled my poor father's old shop. 'We need bigger premises.'

I knew he was right, but my heart wasn't in it any more. I couldn't see it as my whole future. During the days when I was working I was always longing for the evenings when I could get to the clubs or the theatres of the West End. I didn't want to spend the rest of my life wishing I was somewhere else every day.

'Why don't you buy my share of the business, Bernie?' I suggested. 'Then you can do whatever you want with it. I want to go into something else.'

Bernie agreed and we settled on a price of £10,000, which seemed like a huge amount of money. Lily was impressed. Her boy was on the way up and I was still only twenty-one. The 'swinging sixties' were still four years away but I was already living the fantasy. I bought myself a Jaguar XJ 140, a lovely little sports car that had been launched a couple of years before.

Just as Lily had advised, I now had money behind me, and I felt like there was nothing I couldn't do.

★ Romano's ★

It has always seemed obvious to me, maybe because of the lessons I learned at my mother's knee, that if you want something there is no point in sitting around waiting, hoping someone is going to give it to you. It is always better to do it for yourself. It doesn't matter if you are young or inexperienced – those are just excuses for not going out and having a go. Some people make excuses all their lives and end up achieving nothing. Working on that principle even then, I decided that since I loved West End club life, wanted to sing, liked mixing with showbusiness people and had a bit of capital in the bank … I should start a club of my own.

I wanted it to be different from the sort of places I'd been going to with Mike and Bernie, many of which seemed a bit sleazy. I didn't want any hostesses or hookers around the place trying to fleece the punters of money. I also reckoned that when there was a lot of strong competition about, like The Flamingo, which was in Wardour Street, and the famous Whisky A Go Go, I needed to make my place different just to attract the punters.

Since I was still only about twenty-one, most of the other club owners were much older than me, so that was going to make it different to start with because I would be attracting younger people and my taste in music was likely to be different from that of owners and managers who were in their forties or older. I also wanted to set up the sort of sound system that would soon be commonplace everywhere but was then completely new. I wanted a place that played live music most of the time, where people could come to drink and to dance and where they could get food too, although there wouldn't be any formal table service because that would mean hiring waiters and waitresses and increasing the overheads. Above everything, I wanted it to be a fun place where my friends would come and where I could get up on stage myself and sing when the mood took me.

I don't know why I didn't pursue the singing more whole-heartedly at the time. Maybe it just wasn't meant to be, or maybe I didn't want to have my career resting in the hands of other people, which is what always happens to performers one way or another. I guess I was also doing too many other things and wasn't able to concentrate enough. No one makes it big in showbusiness unless they are completely focused and tunnel visioned about their careers.

I found a ground-floor property in Gerrard Street, which is now the pedestrianized centre of Soho's Chinatown, running alongside Shaftesbury Avenue on the other side from Wardour Street and The Flamingo. At that time it was just one more lively and traffic-filled Soho backstreet, and boasted only one Chinese restaurant. The rest of the properties around us were mostly clip joints, where scantily clad ladies persuaded punters to pay inflated prices for inferior drinks, or small traditional shops. All the money I'd got from selling my share of the clothing business to Bernie I sank into refurbishing and stocking the club.

I called it Romano's for no reason beyond the fact that it sounded like the sort of name a sophisticated West End club should have. By the time I had finished there was a big dance floor at the centre of the room, surrounded with tables and chairs. I built a stage at the back and a bar along the side. I installed a state-of-the-art sound system (which would look like something out of the ark now) so that I could play music from a record player whenever the live acts were having their breaks.

No one had thought of hiring disc jockeys at that stage. In fact, I don't think the term had even been invented. It was just me putting records on in the back room. Sometimes we'd have 'special nights', like when I would ask Shan or some other friend to perform. I was beginning to get to know a few of the up-and-coming stars of the time because of her, Mike and Bernie and Stubby Kaye. The resulting atmosphere was all very relaxed and informal, with Mum cooking the food and Dad working behind the bar in the evenings, both of them eager as ever to support me in any way they could and to be involved in the excitement of a new venture.

One of my barmen was a rugged-looking lad called George Sewell, who was a friend of my cousin Bernie, and who went on to become a well-known television actor in police dramas like *Softly Softly* and *Special Branch*. He ended up with Jasper Carrott and Robert Powell, sending himself up in Jasper's television series *The Detectives*. He'd started out with Joan Littlewood's company in the East End, which launched a lot of working-class actors' careers, including Barbara Windsor's. George's brother was a well-known boxer called Danny Sewell, who also went on to be an actor. A lot of East End families had connections with boxing because it was one of the few ways that lads from poor backgrounds could hope to get out and make something of themselves – acting and singing being others, of course.

To get into Romano's you had to be a member and pay a fee, which made it a private club and allowed us to serve drink until one in the morning, after the pubs were closed. Because I was so young and everyone was so friendly I tended to be a bit casual about the rules and I used to let people pay at the door sometimes, which contravened the conditions of our licence. The police got wind of this and decided to do something about it one busy Saturday night. The place was full as always and I was busy, so I didn't notice that a number of people I didn't know had paid on the door to get in. By the time I realized they were all plain-clothes coppers it was too late to deny that we had let things get a bit lax on the door. Mum and Dad were both working there that night and we all had to go down to Bow Street Magistrates' Court to be ticked off and fined. I had learned a lesson and got a bit more careful and professional after that.

One of the biggest potential problems for anyone wanting to open a club, or any other business for that matter, in the West End in the fifties was the attention you would get from gangsters like the infamous Kray twins, who would come looking for protection money as soon as they heard you were open for business. The advantage I had over many Soho traders, however, was that my cousin Bernie used to hang out with some pretty heavy people when he was young, quite fancying the idea of himself as a bit of a gangster for a while. One of his good friends was a guy called Tony Mella, who had a reputation for being a 'hard man'. Tony used to come into the club as a friend and would keep an eye on things for me a bit without asking for any protection money.

We used to get a lot of pretty heavy-duty villains coming in because they were all part of the same social set as the boxing and showbusiness crowd and they were the sort of people who liked to spend their nights in clubs rather than tucked up in bed with their spouses. As a result of Tony being around we hardly ever had any trouble, apart from one night when there was someone in who the other villains had a problem with, so they took him outside and ran over his legs to teach him a lesson for something or other. That was an unusual incident for us – usually everyone got on well. Sooner or later, however, the Krays were bound to get wind of the fact that there might be money to be made from us.

Finally the day arrived. It was about six thirty in the evening and Shan was in my office at the back with Tony Mella sorting some records out for the night ahead. I was around the club somewhere talking to one of my staff when I felt a draught as someone opened the street door. I looked up in time to see Ronnie and Reggie Kray walking towards me, flanked by two of their henchmen. There was no doubt from the scowls on their faces that they had arrived with business in mind. In the few seconds that it took for me to take in what was happening, the door to my office opened and Tony stepped out with Shan. The brothers stopped in their tracks. They stared at Tony and he stared back, none of them moving. None of them spoke, but the Krays turned on their heels and walked straight back out again. We never had any more visits.

Fifty years later I heard from one of my other cousins, David Bloomfield, that the Krays once put on a benefit night for my Uncle Joe, another uncle who was a professional boxer but who didn't get to be as famous as Uncle Jack. I used to spend a lot of time with David and with his sister, Betty, who was a close friend of Mum's. Because I had a different name, I don't think the Krays can have realized that I was related to Joe and Jack and the rest of Mum's family. If they had known I don't believe they would ever have come in looking for business at all. As it was, just seeing Tony there was enough to let them know that they wouldn't be able to intimidate us easily. Eventually Tony got shot in the back by one of his own employees, Big Alf Melvin, in a club he was running called The Bus Stop. Tony reputedly staggered out into Newport Street and died with his head in the lap of a club hostesses, but that wasn't until much later.

Tommy Steele used to come into Romano's nearly every night, and Kenny Lynch, who would later be one of the first black entertainers to make it big in England. Kenny was constantly nagging me to let him sing, but I thought he was just another East End tearaway and kept putting him off with a string of excuses. In the end I relented and let him go up on stage. To my surprise, he was pretty good. Shirley Bassey was in that night and sent him to see her record company, which was the start of his career. He later went on to tour with The Beatles when Helen Shapiro was topping the bill.

Shirley Bassey was even younger than I was. She had started out in a musical based on the life of Al Jolson and another called *Hot From Harlem* and had eventually come to the West End in a show called *Such is Life*. The public became more aware of her when she released a single called 'Burn My Candle (At Both Ends)', which the BBC banned because of its suggestive lyrics, immediately giving her a reputation as a sex symbol. That was followed by a hit called 'The Banana Boat

45

Song' and from thereon she rose steadily to become the great star she still is today.

One evening Shan and I went to a rival club for some dinner and found Kenny Lynch sitting at a table on his own looking particularly agitated.

'I came in with Tommy [Steele]', he told us, 'and he's fucked off and left me with the bill. I can't pay it.'

I paid the bill for him. I think it was probably about £10, and he never forgot it. Tommy had a bit of reputation for disappearing whenever bills appeared. We sometimes used to have poker games back at a flat I rented for myself just round the corner from Romano's after the club closed and Tommy would try to intimidate other players by raising the odds ridiculously high, slapping £50 at a time down on the table. We were all used to his ways. These games were all a lot more high stakes than anything I had seen my family playing during the war years. It wasn't unusual for one or other of us to lose £1,000 in a night, which was a substantial sum then.

Other regular players at those games included Dave Dee, a former policeman who was about to become famous with his group Dave Dee, Dozy, Beaky, Mick and Tich. They had some huge hits like 'The Legend of Xanadu' in which Dave would crack a whip as he sang, dressed as a sort of sixties version of a Regency dandy. He later went behind the scenes and became an A&R (artists and repertoire) man for WEA Records and launched his own label in the early eighties. As a policeman in 1960 he had actually attended the car crash on the A4 in which American guitarist Eddie Cochran ('Summertime Blues', 'C'mon Everybody' and 'Three Steps to Heaven') had been killed, helping to salvage the great man's guitar from the wreckage and reputedly teaching himself to play on it back at the police station. The same guitar, according to legend, had also been carried on that tour for Eddie by a young guy called Mark Feld, another Hackney lad, who changed his name to Marc Bolan, formed the glam rock group T Rex, had huge hits with songs like 'Ride a White Swan', 'Hot Love' and 'Get it On', and also died as a passenger in a car crash in 1977.

Tommy Steele had been on tour with Mike and Bernie when they started to establish themselves in the business and Bernie had started going out with a dancer from the same tour called Siggy. After a show at the Dominion in Tottenham Court Road one Sunday night, Mike, Bernie, two other friends and I went out for dinner to a theatrical restaurant in Soho's Store Street, called Olivelli's. We arrived at about half past twelve and as we went downstairs we saw Siggy sitting at a table with five or six guys who were acrobats from the same show as her at the Prince of Wales Theatre. One of them was a Frenchman, who Bernie thought was getting too close to Siggy.

'There could be trouble here tonight,' I said to Mike as we sat down.

Although we did our best to distract him, we could see that Bernie was getting angrier and angrier and more and more unsettled as the level of laughter rose at the other table. Eventually he couldn't stand it any longer. He stood up and strode over to challenge the Frenchman. We watched as the Frenchman stood up, exchanged angry words with Bernie and then went upstairs with him. The others at their table then got up to follow.

'We'd better go and give him a hand,' Mike said.

Because all the men in our family could box, and because Mum had made sure I was handy with my fists, Mike and I were used to that sort of thing, but the other two guys at our table obviously didn't intend to help out. They probably made the right decision, because it developed into the most enormous street fight, which ended with me being chucked through the restaurant's plate glass window and getting cut to shreds. Mike also did his arm in. The police turned up and they were about to take us all away when our two friends finally emerged from downstairs and managed to convince them that I'd had nothing to do with anything. Because I was a lot smaller than the rest of them the police seemed to be willing to accept that I must be an innocent bystander who had got caught up in something beyond my control. Imagine what a splash the media would make of an incident like that these days if there were a couple of high-profile entertainers like Mike and Bernie involved.

Bernie's unusual courtship methods must have worked because Siggy ended up agreeing to marry him and they had many happy years together.

There were times when things were tough when I used to join forces with Mike and Bernie and practise some of the card playing skills we had learnt from the family as kids, setting up games and making sure we didn't walk away from the tables without some winnings to see us through.

Fights often followed Mike and Bernie around and weren't always their fault. We were going down to the cloakroom of the Stork Club one night just as a group of big, burly blokes came up in the other direction, probably a bit emboldened by drink.

'I didn't know they let bloody Jews in here,' one of the blokes said, at which point Bernie flattened him and another full-scale fight ensued. This time the newspapers did find out and there was a headline on the front page of the London paper the next day. It said 'Gangsters Strike Stork Club'.

All in all, I was having the time of my life. I became engaged to Shan, Romano's was booming, the money was flowing in and I bought myself a beautiful bachelor flat up in Compton Road on the edges of Canonbury and Islington for about £3,000.

One weekend a guy came into the club, having come up to town all the way from Bristol. He was so enamoured by the place he took me to one side and told me he wanted to become my partner.

'Don't be silly,' I said, assuming it was the drink talking.

'No, really,' he insisted. 'I want to be your partner.'

'All right then.' I gave in, thinking I would humour him. 'Give me £1,000 and we'll work out the details later.'

'No,' he went on, 'I want more than that.'

'Then give me fifteen hundred', I said, 'and we'll work out a deal during the week.'

Finally satisfied, he wrote me the cheque, which I duly banked on the Monday, and I never heard from him again. It seemed that when your star was in the ascendant, everyone wanted to be a part of it.

The club was always full of young people who, like me, were looking for ways to make their mark in the world. I had known Barbara Windsor when she was young and lived in Stamford Hill and she often came to the club with a boyfriend who would get up and sing. Another regular was Sean Connery, who was only a few years off landing the part of James Bond. Another was one of the main players in a company called British Land and he tried to persuade me to go into property with him. I turned him down because I was too much in love with the whole showbusiness idea. I think British Land is worth more than £8 billion now, so I definitely could have made a lot more money if I had followed that path – but would I have had as much fun? I doubt it.

★ Riviera to ★
★ Cannes

The experience of creating and running Romano's had whetted my appetite for the whole hospitality business and after a couple of years I was ready to move on to something else, something a bit more upmarket and ambitious. My fast success as a club owner had made me even more full of confidence than I had been after the selling of the fashion business and I thought I could do anything.

I sold Romano's to a guy called Morrie, who owned half a dozen drinking and hostess clubs scattered across the West End, and looked around for something else to invest in. Gerrard Street had been fun but it wasn't the smartest part of town and I wanted a bit more sophistication now. I had always loved eating in restaurants, ever since those Sunday nights when my parents used to take me out to the Trocadero. How hard, I asked myself, could it be to open a place of my own? If only I had asked a few older and wiser people the same question before charging ahead with all the arrogance of youth, then things might have turned out differently.

I found an old car showroom in Hanover Square, one of Mayfair's grandest addresses, in between Bond Street and Regent Street and just below Oxford Street, and I confidently set about converting it into a restaurant. As well as being comfortable in restaurants and clubs in London, I had also been down to the chicest parts of the south of France on holiday by then, and I knew exactly the sort of thing I wanted to create. It would be really smart and there would be some live music as well, so I would still be able to stand up and sing when the urge took me, or invite my new showbusiness friends to do a turn in return for a meal or two. Restaurants were not the commonplace things they are today because most people still didn't have enough disposable income to be able to eat out too often. Most people had not travelled much by then either, so they weren't as familiar with foreign cuisines as they might be today. This was a time when not even Angus Steak Houses had started to appear in London.

I really was starting from scratch with a big empty space, which I had to fit out with everything from a full-scale kitchen to napkins and cutlery. With Romano's I had been able to rely on atmosphere and friendly people and dimmed lights to get away with a few cut corners. Here everything had to be finished to a much higher, and consequently more expensive, standard. It wasn't long before I realized that this mammoth task was going to swallow every penny I had made from selling the club, plus a lot more. Still confident that I knew exactly what I was doing, I decided I needed to raise more money to get everything how I wanted it to be. I started borrowing money, certain I would be able to pay it back once the customers started to flood in the moment we opened our doors.

The restaurant was going to be called Riviera and in my mind it was going to be the height of French sophistication. Because I had been so successful ever since I was eighteen I thought I was invincible, but the restaurant business was something else entirely. There is a big difference between enticing people in to spend a few pounds on drinks in a club and getting them to buy a full-scale meal and then providing something of the standard they are expecting. I had no experience in the catering field beyond getting Mum to cook a few steaks at Romano's, and I had no one around me who could help fill the holes in my knowledge.

Instead of looking for a partner who had experience of the restaurant business, I brought in a friend of my parents, who borrowed some more money to buy his share of the business, with me standing as his personal guarantor. I couldn't have made a bigger or more elemental mistake. He knew no more about upmarket catering than I did and together we lurched from one disaster to the next, the worst one being that we didn't have a drinks licence by the time we opened for business. People going for a posh night out did not take kindly to being told they had to 'bring a bottle'. On top of that, the chef drank too much, the maitre d' we hired had no control over anything, the service was hopeless and I was being robbed blind by virtually everyone involved. It was a nightmare from day one.

By the time the drinks licence came through it was too late. I had lost around £60,000, which in the fifties was an absolute fortune. I was furious with myself for being so arrogant and for biting off more than I could chew. Within a year I had lost everything I had so carefully built up, including my car. I only just managed to hold on to my beloved flat in Canonbury. I had learned a lesson I would never forget: never go into any business you don't completely understand.

Looking back now, I guess I was ten years too early. I had been early with the fashion business as well, but it had worked to my advantage because being on the cutting edge is what fashion is all about, plus my start-up costs were virtually nil. This time I had plunged in way out of my depth and things could only get worse as the outgoings continued to mount and the customers continued to stay away. I needed to find a way to get out quickly without losing even more.

I had met a showman called Paul Raymond who was still only in his early thirties and had just opened his Raymond Revue Bar in the former Doric Ballroom in Soho's Walkers Court. The Revue Bar was for some time by far the classiest strip club in London, probably in the whole of Europe. Paul had started out as an old-fashioned showbusiness impresario before going into the strip club and men's magazines businesses and would eventually have more shows running in the West End than anyone else in history. At the same time he was quietly starting to build a property portfolio around Soho, which would see him becoming one of the country's richest men by the time he died.

I told him my problem and he agreed to take the lease of the Riviera off my hands in exchange for some readies. I was in no position to negotiate and was grateful for anything he was willing to give me. He continued to run the restaurant for a while but didn't do that well either and eventually rented it to Danny la Rue in 1964.

Danny, who was the country's most famous drag artist, had been making a big name for himself in cabaret at clubs like Churchill's and Winstons, impersonating stars like Shirley Bassey, Marlene Dietrich and Carol Channing, all of whom were his friends, and performing a comedy act with Ronnie Corbett. He wanted a venue for a private club of his own where there would be no hostesses so there could be more of a family atmosphere. He proceeded to make the most enormous success of the place, ending up with about 13,000 members. Princess Margaret and her husband Lord Snowdon, who were the most fashionable figures in London at the time, were amongst his regulars, boosting Danny's reputation even further. It was rumoured that he was the highest-paid entertainer in the country for a while. When Danny finally gave up the venue it became the Chicago Pizza Pie Factory.

The swinging sixties were truly getting underway as the years of war and austerity finally started to recede.

Shan, who by this time had become my fiancée, was very supportive as everything crumbled to dust around me, even paying for us to go on holiday together to Sicily. When we got there we decided it was a bit more primitive than we had expected and headed back up to the more familiar territory of the French Riviera. In many countries the tourism industries were still in their infancy in the sixties, with many British people taking their first package holidays to warmer climates. The south of France, however, had been a destination for discerning travellers for a long time.

In Cannes I went to the casino while Shan was asleep, hoping to be able to surprise her with a big win, but I just lost every last penny I had left. It seemed that my winning streak was well and truly over in every way. Shan took the news of my latest loss surprisingly well considering she was already having to pay for everything. Despite my business disappointments we were having some good times together and I did love her.

Shan was on tour in America on the night when I was driving home from a television studio where I had been watching Mike and Bernie recording a show and was suddenly struck with a terrible pain in my stomach. It was so bad that I drove myself straight to University College Hospital where they informed me that my appendix had burst. The doctors operated immediately and apparently it was touch and go for a while as to whether I would make it. But I was lucky and I stayed in the hospital a few days to recuperate. While I was lying in my hospital bed, feeling sorry for myself, a friend came to visit and told me that Shan was having a fling with some American guy on the other side of the Atlantic. I have to admit I hadn't exactly been a saint myself, but that didn't make any difference to how I felt when I heard the news. My male pride couldn't tolerate being two-timed and I called the engagement off.

Now I had no money, no job and no famous fiancée. I knew I had to do something to get my life back on track but I had no idea what that something should be. I certainly didn't fancy getting a regular job after being my own boss for so long. When I met a guy in a bar who was working for an American company selling *The Encyclopedia Americana* it sounded like a possible short-term solution to my cash-flow problem. Hadn't I proved in the past that I was a great salesman?

'They don't pay you a salary,' he warned, 'but you can make great commission. We sell mainly to American servicemen.'

I took the job and travelled around to the American bases with my new best friend, knocking on the doors of American soldiers. We sold a few individual encyclopedias but the main aim was to sell a yearbook, which would mean the customers were signed up to pay $10 a year for the rest of their lives. It wasn't a terrible way to spend your days, and at least it gave me enough to live on.

'We should go down to Cannes,' my colleague suggested, 'because the American Sixth Fleet comes in there and the sailors come ashore in droves.'

I was always happy for any excuse to go down to the Riviera, but after a month or so of hustling on the streets and in the bars, I realized that when sailors come ashore on leave in a place like Cannes the last thing on their minds is buying sets of encyclopedias. I was going to need a gimmick if I was going to make any sales at all.

I had been eating at a restaurant in the harbour called Le Parrot and I noticed that the upstairs was always empty during the day. I asked the owner if I could use it and he agreed with the usual Gallic shrug of disinterest. Instead of selling to servicemen on a one-to-one basis, I thought I should find a way of getting ten or twenty of them in at a time so I could present to them simultaneously.

I had a French girlfriend who I had met down there, so I recruited her and a few of her friends to hand out leaflets offering free beer to servicemen who would like to come to Le Parrot and meet me. Men tend to be politer to pretty girls who accost them in the street than they would be to other men, and they were happy to accept a free beer, so I found I could quite easily fill the room, make my pitch with a fake American accent and start getting sales. I had a magnificent white leather Bible with illustrations and a section that they could dedicate to their families.

'Gentlemen,' I would say with all the hammy solemnity of a born-again preacher, 'I would like to ask you to stand for our Lord Jesus.'

As they all stood I would open the book and hold it up to them.

'I'm sure you all have someone back at home who would like this Bible. Your mother maybe, or your sweetheart, or your wife. I am going to give one of these to each and every one of you today once you come into the *Encyclopedia Americana* ...'

Though I say it myself, I was good. I used to sign up five or six of them at a time, taking as little as two dollars off them on the spot, but getting those precious signatures and serial numbers, because once I had those I had them committed for life. But even as I was closing the sales and racking up the commission I knew this wasn't how I should be spending my life and after a few months I decided I had to come back to England and try to get back on my feet again. I'd cleared all my debts by then and had a few pounds in my pocket, but I still didn't know what I was going to do next.

Arriving back in London I went to see my parents and they told me that they had a neighbour upstairs called Lou Lewis who wanted to talk to me. Willing to explore every possible avenue, I went up and introduced myself.

'I hear you're good at manufacturing,' Lou said.

'I'm good at the design and concept side of it all,' I replied.

'Well, I believe people really want to buy leatherwear,' he said. 'Why don't you come into business with me?'

The idea didn't make my heart sing, but I remembered that I had done well in the manufacturing business before, so maybe that was what I was meant to do. Maybe I needed to be sensible and start putting my life straight. I agreed to give it a go. We rented a little factory in the East End and opened a showroom, but almost immediately I knew I was in the wrong place. This was not how I wanted to spend the rest of my life. I had so enjoyed running the club, socializing amidst the glamour of the West End, and the excitement of the early stages of trying to get the restaurant going, and I also enjoyed being around Mike and Bernie and Shan and the other showbusiness people who had become my friends. Those were the worlds I wanted to move in all the time, but what should I do about it?

I had to come clean with Lou and admit I'd made a mistake. I had to think of something else to do.

I often ended up meeting interesting people from my mother's life, mainly because she was so outgoing and always got to know everything about her neighbours or anyone else she bumped into in the course of her day. One of her neighbours in Highbury Grove Court, the Islington block she and Dad lived in, was Don Black. He had recently got married to Shirley, who he is still with forty or more years later, and was already deeply involved in the showbusiness world that I found so fascinating. Before he hit the big time as a songwriter Don was an office

57

boy with a music publishing firm, a song-plugger and an agent. He worked for Vic Lewis, a famous jazz guitarist and band-leader who later became an agent as well, working with Brian Epstein on The Beatles' American tour and managing Cilla Black, Shirley Bassey and Matt Munro, the biggest names of their time. In the end Brian Epstein bought Vic out and put him on the board of his company. After Brian died Vic went on to sign Elton John before changing track in the mid seventies and working with the Royal Philharmonic Orchestra, finally returning to his first love: jazz. All the musical styles were mixed together in those days, and the same people would keep cropping up in all different walks of the business.

The world first realized Don's songwriting abilities when he wrote the lyrics for the theme music to the 1965 James Bond film *Thunderball*, which led to *Diamonds are Forever* and the *Man with the Golden Gun*, all of which he wrote in collaboration with the composer John Barry. Don then went on to write *Tomorrow Never Dies* and *The World is Not Enough* with David Arnold. His most famous song, however, would be 'Born Free', for the 1966 film about Elsa the lion, which Don also wrote with John Barry. The credits kept on rolling after that, including 'Ben' for Michael Jackson and musicals like *Billy*, *Tell Me on a Sunday* and *Aspects of Love*. The artists who he had worked with in management, like Shirley Bassey and Matt Munro, became synonymous with his greatest hits.

Don also had a brother, Michael, who was as wild and flamboyant as Don was reserved and dignified, and who was also an agent. Many years later Michael would marry Julie Rogers, a singer who had an immense hit in the early sixties with 'The Wedding', after meeting her at my house when they were both guests at the bar mitzvah of my eldest son, Oliver.

Right from the beginning I liked the sound of Don and Michael's lives, just like I enjoyed being with Mike and Bernie, but I still couldn't see how I could get into the same sort of business myself. Like many young people, my fantasy was still to be a singer, but I didn't seem to be focused enough to get a career going in that area. I had seen how much work the Kaye Sisters had had to put into staying on top and I was too easily distracted by other things. There had to be another answer – but what?

★ Breaking ★ into ★ Showbusiness ★

By the time the sixties were underway I was in my late twenties and I really needed to get myself sorted out if I wasn't going to get left behind as everyone else became rich and successful around me. I was still very close with my cousins, Mike and Bernie, who had become big comedy stars by then, having settled into their double act with Bernie as the goofy comic and Mike the straight man. They had even starred on the *Royal Variety Show* and *Sunday Night at the London Palladium*, which were the biggest variety shows in the country at the time. Television was beginning to get a firm grip on the nation's attention and was making household names and faces of people like Mike and Bernie, Jimmy Tarbuck and Bruce Forsyth in a way that live theatre could never achieve. In a theatre a comic might perform to several thousand people at a time, many of whom would be watching from quite a distance. Now they were watched by as many at twenty million people at a time and the cameras meant that everyone could get to know what the performers looked like in close-up, removing all hope of privacy and anonymity should you want it, a situation that film stars had been growing used to for forty years or more. I guess this was the birth of the celebrity-obsessed society that we have today, where every pimple and blemish on a celebrity body will be featured in a magazine somewhere, every drunken mishap or family dispute making it on to the front pages.

I was round at Bernie's house for dinner one evening when the delicate subject of my future came up.

'So, what are you going to do with your life, Merv?' he asked, like a concerned big brother.

'I don't know,' I admitted. 'I seem to be going round in circles.'

'Joe wants to set up a rock and roll side to the business,' he said. 'Would you like me to have a word?'

'That would be like a life's dream for me,' I said.

Joe Collins was their agent and I knew of him from when I was running Romano's and used to listen in to people like Shirley Bassey talking about the business. Joe later wrote about his first meeting with Shirley, when he interviewed her in his office. 'She was just a skinny little thing in her mid teens,' he wrote, 'yet I sensed she had stage presence and could be made to look stylish. I did not bother to hear her sing. I reckoned that even if she wasn't much good as a vocalist, she would fit my show if she were dressed the way I had in mind.' It's not hard to imagine Simon Cowell saying something similar about any of his acts these days.

Mike and Bernie had been introduced to Joe by our Uncle Mick, the publican who went on to live with Mum and Dad, who had met Joe around the West End. Everyone in the business knew everyone else in those days because there simply weren't as many people around.

Joe was more than thirty years older than me and one of the biggest agents in London. As well as Mike and Bernie and Shirley, he represented all sorts of other stars, like Dorothy Squires (Roger Moore's first wife and a big singing star of the time). He was also the father of Joan Collins, who was a year or so older than me, and Jackie, who was a couple of years younger.

At that stage Joan had already been signed up by 20th Century Fox as their answer to MGM's Elizabeth Taylor, and she was already famous for being a pin-up girl (a role that did not involve anything like nudity or even going topless – all that was still to come). Jackie had also followed the family tradition and become an actress, although her heart wasn't in it to quite the same extent as Joan's and she would soon publish her first book, *The World is Full of Married Men*, which would launch her on a career as one of the world's most successful novelists. This was a family that was seriously enmeshed in the world of entertainment that I enjoyed so much. I couldn't imagine anything better than being able to work with, and learn from, a man like Joe Collins.

Joe had come from the same sort of Jewish family as mine, brought up around the markets of Petticoat Lane. Music hall and vaudeville had run in his family for several generations and Joe had been enormously successful as an agent and was the former partner of Lew and Leslie Grade. He had actually started as Lew's agent when Lew was a professional dancer, before going into partnership with him. By the time I knew them Lew had moved on to become one of the most powerful men in commercial television, having produced the long-running series *The Saint*, which had starred Roger Moore, and *Sunday Night at the London Palladium*. He owned part of the company that produced all the big puppet television shows of the time, like *Thunderbirds*. He later commissioned Jim Henson to create *The Muppets* and created the *Pink Panther* movie franchise with Peter Sellers's famous portrayal of the bumbling Inspector Clouseau. As well as owning Associated Television (ATV), Lew also had Pye Records, a talent agency, and Northern Music, a publishing company he bought from Dick James. Northern Music owned all The Beatles' songs, and Elton John's, although the latter relationship ended up in court. I remember Dick taking Elton John down to Midem in the south of France when the young singer-songwriter was still virtually unknown and staging a concert that pretty much launched him.

Dick was another man who had been steeped in the old world of showbusiness that men like Joe and Lew had emerged from. Born Reginald Leon Isaac Vapnick in 1920, he started out as a singer with north London dance bands. He was a regular performer at the Cricklewood Palais when he was still only seventeen. He sang with the Henry Hall Band and Geraldo's. He sang the theme tune of the original *Robin Hood* television series in the fifties, which must have been one of the best-known and catchiest theme tunes ever recorded.

So, Joe Collins had been living and working at the very heart of showbusiness ever since the days of vaudeville. Wily enough to know that rock and roll was going to be the next big thing to fill both London and provincial theatres, he had just agreed to put on the first Beatles' Christmas Show, but he was also wise enough to know that he was not of the right age either to enjoy the music or understand the rock and roll culture. He had heard his two younger kids, Jackie and Bill, playing records at home (and Jackie was also quite friendly with Tommy Steele), but in Joe's opinion the kids who made the records were 'scruffy, unprofessional amateurs' and he didn't really want to have to deal with them himself.

'They don't rehearse', he would complain, 'and they won't even be told how to walk on to a stage properly. Furthermore, I can't stand the noise they make!'

He needed someone from Jackie and Bill's generation to do the same in the rock and roll field as he had done in variety. I'm sure he would have liked to keep the business in the family and to have handed the job to his son, but Bill, Joan and Jackie's younger brother, was a very private man and was not interested in carrying on the family's high-profile theatrical traditions.

I used to see Joe at the Arsenal as well, where he was just as avid a supporter of the team as I was, so when I went to see him for the first time I was confident that we would get on. Sure enough, we did. Years later I found out that Bernie had told him to give me the job and I expect Joe thought that he had nothing to lose by agreeing to do his star client a favour, and that if I didn't work out he would be able to get rid of me as quickly as he had taken me on, without unduly endangering his relationship with Mike and Bernie. He agreed to give me fifty per cent of any business I handled, starting with the Beatles' Christmas Show at the Finsbury Park Astoria, plus my expenses.

Whatever his reasons for agreeing to give me a chance, it was the luckiest break I had ever had. It would have taken me years to have made the contacts that Joe was able to pass on to me. In fact I doubt I would ever have been able to do it on my own at that age. Many of the people who ran the theatres were Joe's age, and already at the top of the theatrical profession. He knew them all and was happy to tell them they should see me.

Joe also introduced me to the Variety Club, which does so much great work for disadvantaged children. It became one of my favourite charities from that moment onwards and I ended up serving on many of its committees in later years.

Once they know you have the backing of someone like Joe, people are willing to give you a chance. He had one friend, for instance, called Cyril Lavant who owned a theatre in the Isle of Wight where he wanted to put on rock and roll shows. Joe simply introduced us and told me to handle it, throwing me in at the deep end while letting me know that he would be there if I ever needed advice.

In those days an agent needed to understand exactly how each theatre worked, what the seating capacities were like, the lighting facilities, the dressing rooms – everything that might eventually impact on what sort of show you could stage there and the amount of money that show would take. There were still hundreds of venues for live music around the country, not just theatres but ballrooms and drinking clubs as well, particularly up north, all of them needing acts to draw the punters in. There were at least seven or eight clubs in Manchester alone where they put big shows on.

The people who owned the venues needed the people who managed the talent as much as the other way round. In the West End the balance of power was slightly different because so many people wanted to get into those theatres, so the owners could pick and choose, but at the same time there were opportunities where a theatre would suddenly fall empty and the owners would be looking around for a show that was already up and running somewhere else in the country and could be moved quickly to the West End.

Joe had a great office in Chandos Place, just off St Martin's Lane, above an arch going in behind the Coliseum Theatre. Paul Raymond, the guy who had saved me by buying the Hanover Square restaurant, was renting attic space off him upstairs as he set about laying the foundations of his Soho property empire. Paul was still touring strip shows around the country where the girls had to stay stock still if they didn't want to be arrested for indecency. He actually tried to persuade Joe to invest in the Revue Bar when it first opened, but Joe turned him down, expecting the place to be closed down by the police before it had a chance to make a profit. Joe couldn't have predicted how completely everything was going to change in the coming years. Paul was very much a man in the right place at the right time.

I moved into an office next to Joe's, which I shared with an older man called Cyril Gibbons who used to do all the administrative jobs for Joe's pantomimes, like hiring the chorus girls. I liked Cyril and carefully watched the way he worked, learning all the time. (It was in one of Joe's pantomimes that Danny la Rue first got to do his drag act. Before then he had been an all-round entertainer, but Joe cast him and his partner, Allen Hayes, as Cinderella's ugly sisters at theatres in Gloucester and York, paying them £90 a week between them, and that was how Danny found that he had a talent for wearing glamorous frocks and making people laugh at the same time.)

I set up Mervyn Conn Promotions and starting booking acts and organizing my own tours. They were different from the sort of acts Joe would be interested in, but in many ways the variety format was just the same. The first show I did I split my fifty per cent with Phil Solomon, an Irish Jew who owned the pirate radio station Radio Caroline and had his own record label, Major Minor Records. Radio Caroline had started broadcasting in 1964 from a ship anchored three miles offshore. Tony Benn, who was then Home Secretary, eventually managed to get the pirates closed down four years later in 1968, but by then the British public had developed a taste for non-stop music and the BBC was forced to launch Radio One in 1967. Disc jockeys like Tony Blackburn, Dave Lee Travis and Johnnie Walker who had started on Caroline then became legitimate BBC stars.

Despite having to share my earnings, my first show still made me just over £500 profit. The Bachelors, the Irish trio who had been discovered and managed by Phil Solomon and his wife, Dorothy, were top of the bill. I've still got the accounts book where I wrote everything down: £35 for Elkie Brookes, £85 for my old mate Kenny Lynch, who had been on tour with The Beatles by then and had had a couple of hits with 'Up On The Roof' and 'You Can Never Stop Me Loving You'. He had also released a version of the Beatles' 'Misery', which had flopped, but got him a lot of publicity. There are other shows in the book too. The Who, for instance, did their first ever professional show for me in Oxford, for which I gave them £30. Georgie Fame and the Blue Flames were big at the time and so I had to pay them £250.

Many of the new groups and singers who were coming along were very exciting, but we had no idea how permanently everything was going to change and we went on staging the shows as they always had been staged, giving the public what they expected.

There are basically four different ways of structuring a deal if you are an impresario. The first is to rent the theatre, the second is a percentage deal, the third is a 'first call' and the fourth is a guarantee against a percentage. People think that when a ticket is sold the money goes to the impresario or producer, but he or she is actually the last one to draw money. Everyone else gets a bite of the cherry first and then whatever is left at the end is the producer's. If the show is a huge hit, of course, like *Mamma Mia* or *Phantom of the Opera*, that can end up being a lot of money, but if it closes quickly the producers will lose whatever money they have put into it. As I became more experienced I tended not to have outside investors for most of the shows I was involved with, preferring to take the brunt of the risk myself.

Joe's timing was impeccable because The Beatles were going stratospheric in 1963 with huge hits like 'She Loves

You' and 'Twist and Shout' and the media was full of stories about 'Beatlemania', which was stoking up the hysteria and leading to tens of thousands of young girls turning up wherever there was even a rumour that John, George, Paul and Ringo would be. The shows they were doing, however, still had more to do with old-fashioned variety and music hall entertainments than modern rock tours as we know them now, but the audiences were very different from anything the theatres were used to, made up of hysterical fans who just wanted to be near their heroes, to see them and to scream at them. The group was supported by other acts including Rolf Harris, Cilla Black (another of Brian Epstein's discoveries) and the Barron Knights (who did very successful comedy songs and impressions of other groups and singers), and there were some comedy sketches for the boys to perform in amongst the songs.

The sketches had to be pretty visual because no one could hear anything over the screaming of the fans. It was just one long, ear-shattering, hysterical shriek from start to finish and at the end of each show we would find at least a hundred pairs of girls' knickers lying discarded amongst the seats. No one had ever seen anything like it before and none of us had any idea how this new trend would develop. Was it just a passing phase? Would people grow tired of the gimmick and go back to the more traditional forms of entertainment? Being younger than many of the other people working in the business, I tended to think not, but still I couldn't have predicted that The Beatles, or at least Paul McCartney, would still be selling out venues like the O2 over forty years later and still commanding worldwide adoration.

The first Christmas show was a complete sell out, all 100,000 seats filled, and we were contracted to do another 38-show run the following year at the Odeon in Hammersmith. We just hoped they would still be as popular after another year. We needn't have worried. By the time the first Christmas show was finishing its run in January 1964, 'I Wanna Hold Your Hand' was entering the American charts and The Beatles were about to go global.

In Hammersmith we booked Jimmy Savile, who had been catapulted to national fame when he presented the first edition of *Top of the Pops* on New Year's Day in 1964, and we put a number of other acts on bill with The Beatles again, including Freddie and the Dreamers and the Yardbirds (who had a young guitarist in their lineup called Eric Clapton).

Even after The Beatles had become world superstars the boys stayed true to their original personalities, which is probably one of the reasons why the fans stayed with them. There was an artists' bar at Hammersmith where we all used to hang out and John, George and Ringo were always happy to buy anyone a drink. Paul, on the other hand, was always careful to keep his hand in his pocket, so much so that it became a running joke amongst the band's entourage.

Not all the acts I worked with were as professional and easy to work with as The Beatles. When he was at the height of his popularity I built up a full-scale tour for PJ Proby, which turned into an infamous media nightmare. I first met PJ through an agent called Tony Lewis, who I had met in unfortunate circumstances a few years before, when I was engaged to Shan. I had driven down to Brighton to pick her up from the Hippo-drome where she was performing. As I waited for her to come out of the theatre I saw her kissing a guy I didn't recognize. Having been brought up all my life amongst people who tended to hit first and ask questions later, I went straight up and punched the poor unsuspecting guy on the nose. He turned out to be Tony Lewis. Once it had been explained to me that they were just friends saying goodnight, Tony and I became good friends. I discovered that he worked for a theatrical agent called John Hayman who was very important at the time, handling, amongst others, Elizabeth Taylor and Richard Burton, who were pretty much the biggest stars in the world. Every newspa-per was full of tales of their infamous rows and of the fabulous jewels he would buy her.

I was actually in the office once when the great couple were there, shouting and screaming at one another at the tops of their voices. Burton broke off for a moment and turned to me. 'We don't always behave like this,' he said, before going straight back to screaming at his wife.

My mother was on the *QE II* with them once, on her way back from New York. She happened to be walking past their stateroom when she heard them shouting through an open door. She knocked and walked right in.

'You two,' she said, scolding them like they were her own children. 'You are such a lovely couple, you really shouldn't row like this all the time. You've made so many wonderful films.'

No doubt they were taken completely by surprise, but ended up inviting her to sit down for a drink and a chat and they stayed friendly for the rest of the trip.

When Tony told me he had signed PJ Proby and played me some of his music I thought he had a really great voice and suggested that I should organize a British tour for him. Tony jumped at the idea and I booked his newest star into venues all over the country from the Odeon Bolton to Kettering Granada, Finsbury Park Astoria to Birmingham Odeon. I could always be confident of getting good deals from the Odeon Group, having brought them The Beatles.

Proby was on about £3,000 a night, which was really big money then, but he was worth it because he'd had a few giant hits by then – the ballad 'Somewhere' and the faster-paced 'Hold Me' and 'Together'. I had to pay his orchestra another £400 a night as well, and there were obviously a lot of other expenses, so I had a lot riding on the tour being a hit. This was the period when the tours were finally changing from the traditional variety model of having a number of different acts on the same bill to having one headliner and a support act, which is pretty much the structure most tours still have today. Tickets were selling well and there seemed to be no reason to worry any more than usual. PJ was a good-looking guy with a big female fan base and he used to wear tight velvet trousers with no underpants, as well as tying his long hair back in a bow, like some Regency fop. Anyone, however, who has ever worn tight velvet will be aware that there's no give in the material and the first night he went on stage he split the

70

trousers and everything came tumbling out. It is hard to imagine in these days of endless publicity stunts how shocking such an event was at the time, getting him on to the front pages of all the papers. Although a few people were shocked and saw it as indicative of the degenerative effect of pop music on young people, most treated it as funny and as a genuine mishap. The second night of the tour, of course, the press were all in, taking pictures, and guess what: he did it again.

Suddenly there were people who were not so amused, particularly the people from the theatre chains like Rank who had him booked in for later in the tour and were frightened he was going to do the same in their premises, getting them into trouble with local authorities, maybe even jeopardizing their licences. They started calling Joe, who also did not like the idea of having his good name besmirched in a business where goodwill and reputation meant everything.

'What the fuck is going on with this guy?' Joe demanded to know. 'Go and tell him that he can't behave like this in the theatre.'

We had a lot at stake on this tour and I was getting nervous even before Joe intervened. Tony, who was also aware that his client was in danger of getting himself blacklisted in every theatre in the country, headed down with me to the grand house where PJ was staying in Mayfair's Hill Street. We were supposed to meet him at eleven o'clock in the morning but there was no sign of him when we arrived and he eventually came strolling downstairs at about twelve thirty with a bottle of Chivas Regal in one hand, a glass in the other and a young woman looped over his arm. It seemed he was taking his role as 'bad boy rock star' very seriously.

'Hi, guys,' he slurred as he flopped on to a sofa. 'Great show last night.'

'Great show, PJ,' I agreed. 'That's what I want to talk to you about.'

'What's that, Mervyn?'

'PJ, you can't split the trousers again tonight at the Granada Tooting, because if you do the tour is off and they'll drop the

71

iron curtain on you. You've got every main theatre controller coming in tonight to check the show out.'

'Mervyn,' he said, putting a reassuring arm around my shoulder, 'you have my word I won't ever do that again.'

I passed Joe the good news and we both decided we had better be in Tooting that night to make sure that he did as he had promised. Not surprisingly, the theatre was packed, and we could see all the theatre controllers at the back, their faces looking grim. Sure enough, PJ did it again, to the exasperation of everyone involved, and that was the end of the tour. It was also pretty much the end of PJ's career as a big star, although he has never been forgotten by those of us who were around at the time. In those days there was no way round the theatrical establishment, not like there is nowadays, with the internet and thousands of independent ways to reach the punters. Back then, the owners of the live venues and record companies held all the cards. If they lost faith in you or decided you were too big a risk that was the end of it. There were always plenty of other acts waiting in the wings who were willing to stick to the rules and behave professionally.

Our immediate problem then was how were we going to fill all the theatres that we had booked for him to perform at? We still had to pay the owners and if we had to return all the ticket money we could end up losing a huge amount. I needed to find another act that could step into the breach instantly.

There was a young guy called Tom Jones, who was then number one in the charts with 'It's Not Unusual', a song written for him by his manager, Gordon Mills, and Les Reed. Mills was a very successful operator and had also come up with the name 'Jones' (Tom was actually christened Thomas Woodward). He wasn't anything like as big or controversial a star as Proby at that time, but I was pretty sure he appealed to a similar sector of the market. I rang Tom's agent and asked if he would like to replace PJ on the tour. It must have seemed like a good break for him at the time because he was delighted to step in and he was as great as you would expect, and totally professional. Because he wasn't as big a star, we did lose some money in ticket sales, but not nearly as much as we would have

72

done if we'd had to cancel the whole thing and leave the theatres empty. Tom's professionalism has stood him in good stead and goes a long way to explaining why he is still such an enormous star more than forty years later.

Gordon Mills had a roommate at one time, a singer called Gerry Dorsey. After his success with Tom, Gordon took on the management of Gerry, suggested he changed his name to Englebert Humperdinck and released a record of him singing a popular old ballad, 'Release Me', which had been written about twenty years earlier. It resulted in one of the biggest-selling records ever, keeping the Beatles' 'Strawberry Fields Forever' off the number-one spot and staying in the charts for something like fifty-six weeks, selling eight-five thousand copies a day at its height. When people look back at the music of the sixties they tend to remember the psychedelia and the experimental stuff and forget that it was standards like 'Release Me' that were actually the biggest sellers.

Many, many years later, when I was organizing the giant country festival at Wembley, a call came through to my secretary.

'There's a Mr PJ Proby on the phone for you, Mr Conn,' she told me. 'Do you want to speak to him?'

'Sure.'

'Mervyn?' the familiar voice came drawling down the line. 'It's PJ here. Remember me?'

'PJ,' I said, 'how could I ever forget you?'

'Mervyn, I want you to realize one thing. I'm a great country singer.'

'You are a great singer, PJ. What can I do for you?'

'Well, you run a big country music festival, Mervyn, and I would like to get on the show.'

'PJ,' I said. 'Get yourself a pair of trousers. Bye.'

I felt better after that.

★ American ★
★ Travels

I used to go a lot to the Ad Lib Club, which was on the fourth floor at 7 Leicester Place, just off Leicester Square, back at the heart of the West End that my family had known so well for so long. All the stars used to go to the Ad Lib, including The Beatles, The Stones and The Kinks, as well as fashion designers like Mary Quant, film stars like Julie Christie and young royals like Princess Margaret. Rumour has it that John Lennon and George Harrison tripped on LSD there for the first time after someone dropped loaded sugar cubes into their drinks at a private house where they had been having dinner earlier that night.

The club had been opened by Oscar Lerman, a real gentleman who went on not only to marry Joe Collins' younger daughter, Jackie, but also to start another club called Dolly's and then the world-famous Tramp with Johnny Gold, which became the ultimate jet-set club during the seventies and is still going today. Ringo Starr proposed to his first wife, Maureen, at the Ad Lib and courted his second wife, Barbara Bach, at Tramp.

Johnny Gold (Oscar's business partner) and his father were my bookmakers in the days before they were allowed to have betting shops. I used to ring them up to place bets, and then one day Johnny told me he was opening a new club and I became a founder member of Tramp.

The Ad Lib didn't last very long, but during my time there I got very friendly with a young guy called Marshall Chess. Marshall was American and his father and uncle had founded Chess Records, a Chicago-based independent record label that had an incredible list of artists including Muddy Waters, Howlin' Wolf, Bo Diddley and Chuck Berry. I had a stunning-looking friend called Bernice Swanson, an actress and cover girl who also wanted to be a singer. She didn't have a particularly good voice but Marshall fell madly in love with her and asked me to be her manager so that he could be the man behind the scenes in her career.

'I would have to ask Joe,' I said, and it was arranged for Marshall to bring Bernice into the office. She was very flamboyant, throwing herself all over the place, and Joe wasn't impressed, so we just let the opportunity slip past, but I stayed friendly with Marshall.

Because we were being so successful with the tours in England, Joe realized rock and roll was here to stay and asked me what I would like to do to broaden the base of the business. He and I were getting on like a father and son by then. He was teaching me so much, taking off a lot of the rough edges to my personality, and we shared so many passions, from showbusiness to Arsenal. He had learned to trust me and showed a lot of faith in my judgment when it came to things that these days would probably be described as 'youth culture'.

'I would really like to go to America,' I said. 'But I don't want to rush in and out. I want to spend some time there and go to New York and to Chicago and to Los Angeles.'

I was thinking that I could stay with Marshall in Chicago and during my dealings with The Beatles I had become good friends with Tony Barrow and Derek Taylor, two ex journalists who had been handling all the group's press and publicity and were part of their inner circle. Derek was living in Los Angeles and I thought I would make contact with him over there and he could show me around town. Although the British acts were then the biggest in the world (ever since the arrival of The Beatles, The Stones and all the rest), for me America was still been the cradle of rock and roll, having produced stars like Elvis, Bill Haley and Chubby Checker, and it still represented the biggest potential marketplace for artists of all sorts. I felt I now understood the British market and I wanted to broaden my experience and become more international. Joe was happy to go along with that, and I bought myself a ticket.

I arrived first in New York, excited to finally be on American soil after a lifetime of watching American films and listening to American music. I met up with a guy called Dick Allen who worked for Universal Attractions, a big agency that is still going today, representing people like MC Hammer and The Stylistics. On our second meeting Dick suggested I come with him to see James Brown in concert. I had heard a lot about the man, but never had a chance to see him, so I readily agreed. As we were about to leave the office Dick went to his drawer and pulled out a gun, discreetly slipping it into his pocket.

'What's that for?' I asked, shocked. Guns were still a virtual unknown on the streets of London. Even the police still relied on their trusty truncheons to keep order.

'Well,' he shrugged, 'we're going to the Apollo in Harlem.'

By then the Apollo was one of the most famous music hall venues in America, having launched hundreds of black acts, including Ella Fitzgerald as far back as 1934. I didn't fully know what I was in for as I hadn't dealt with many black artists by that stage. This was still an era when *The Black and White Minstrel Show* was a major Saturday night television attraction in Britain, with the white male singers wearing crude black make-up and giving the most blatant Al Jolson–Uncle Tom-style performances, while the girls remained resolutely white. Black music was still a culture the British were very ignorant about and it was virtually impossible to get audiences into live venues to see most black performers, apart from the great names of jazz. Hoping to change that, Berry Gordy, the founder of the Motown record label, had brought over some of his young artists to tour, including The Supremes, Stevie Wonder and The Four Tops. I went to see the show at the Finsbury Park Astoria. It was great, but there was hardly anyone in the audience. As always, success is all about timing.

When we got to the theatre Dick and I were the only white faces in the whole place, standing at the back, excited and nervous in equal measure. The atmosphere was fantastic but I found it hard to forget that my companion thought it necessary to pack a gun until the moment when James Brown himself burst out on to the stage and I could think of nothing else but his performance. The man's energy and showmanship and the way he carried the audience with him was *incredible*. I'd never seen anything like it and I could see that this sort of music was going to be the way the rest of the world would soon be going, even if they didn't yet know it. I tried many times to book him to come to Britain, but I never managed it.

On that first American trip I booked Chubby Checker, the guy who popularized 'the twist', Martha Reeves and the Vandellas (as in 'Jimmy Mack' and 'Dancing in the Street') and Bo Diddley, known as 'the Originator' for his role in the transition of blues music to rock and roll and for his influence over the next generation of great artists including Hendrix, Clapton and Buddy Holly.

The first time I met Bo in a hotel room he made his feelings very clear.

'I don't stand any shit, you know,' he growled, staring at me challengingly from under hooded eyes.

'What do you mean?' I asked innocently.

'I want my money and I want it before I go on every night. I'm a black man,' he said, vigorously rubbing the skin on the back of his wrist as if I needed convincing, 'and I don't like the white folk fucking me around.'

'I'm not going to fuck you around for your money, Bo,' I assured him. 'You can have your money before each show.'

His attitude was understandable, because in the late sixties there were still many areas of America where black people had to sit at the back of the buses and go into restaurants through different entrances. The reality of the situation hit home to me particularly hard when I went to Nashville for the first time in 1968, where attitudes were still very entrenched.

At the time of my first trip to America I was going out with a girl called Sue, who was secretary to the comic actor Norman Wisdom. When he heard that I was going to New York Norman gave me a script for a play that he wanted to get on to Broadway. He'd already had some success there in a show called *Stop the World, I Want to Get Off*, but there had been a lot of confrontations between him and Tony Newley (who was Joe Collins' son-in-law for a while, during a high-profile marriage to Joan). Norman wanted me to meet a producer called Marty Erlichman and show him the play. I did as he suggested and Marty invited me to the opening of his new show, *Funny Girl*. Not having any idea what it was going to be about I went to the show and witnessed Barbra Streisand's debut performance. It was one of the greatest theatrical experiences I had ever had, a true 'star is born' moment.

Marty suggested that I take Norman's script to Los Angeles with me to show a friend of his who was starting out in the movies. Nothing came of it, which didn't please Norman, who thought I had let him down. He was not an easy man to deal with, a far cry in reality from the little slapstick clown that the public loved so much.

In Chicago I met Marshall's father, Leonard Chess, and was shown round all the sights of the city, including the bullet holes left by characters like Dillinger only thirty or so years before. Marshall was still determined to persuade me that I should manage Bernice and I was finding it difficult to come up with any more convincing excuses.

'I'll need some money to go down that route,' I said eventually, thinking that would put an end to the discussion once and for all.

'No problem,' Marshall said, writing out a cheque for $5,000 and passing it over. 'You're going to Las Vegas on your way to LA aren't you?'

'Yes, I am.'

'Cash the cheque there,' he said. 'I'll make arrangements for you at Caesar's Palace. But don't lose the money at the tables.'

'I won't lose the money,' I assured him, and we both laughed at the idea. But of course when I got there I couldn't resist the lure of the green baize and I did lose the lot. The gambling streak in my blood was never far from the surface.

A few years later, after the death of his father, Marshall left Chess Records and became the Founding President of Rolling

Stones Records, the group's own label, and poor Bernice never did get to become a star. Some things are just not meant to be.

I travelled on to LA from Las Vegas and was invited to stay in Beverly Hills by a woman I'd met in London, who had been going out with Mick Jagger for a while. I took up the invitation, but she seemed to think that we would be 'good together' on a permanent basis, so I did a runner and went looking for Derek Taylor. I still didn't feel ready to commit to a full-time relationship: too many other things to think about, too many other things to do.

Derek had told me he was managing a new group called The Byrds, who he said were very heavily influenced by The Beatles. They were playing at a famous music venue in West Hollywood called The Troubadour, which was where any number of acts from Elton John to James Taylor got their early breaks. It was also the place where Lenny Bruce, the famous satirist and stand-up comedian, had been arrested on obscenity charges; comedian Richard Pryor later recorded his first live album; Carly Simon, while opening for Cat Stevens, met her future husband James Taylor for the first time; and Lori Lieberman wrote 'Killing Me Softly' after seeing Don McLean perform there. Derek took me along to hear his protégés and I could immediately tell that he was right: they were very talented and had a totally new sound.

'Book 'em for a tour of England,' Derek said.

'But no one knows them in England,' I protested. 'How would I sell tickets?'

'We've got a record coming out that will change all that,' he said. 'I'm telling you, Merv, book 'em now and you'll get 'em cheap. They're going to be *huge*.'

I trusted Derek's judgement, but I still rang Joe to check he didn't think I was making a mistake. It was going to take a big leap of faith to book theatres with an unknown act and hope they would have a hit before they walked out on stage.

'I think they are really good,' I told Joe. 'It could be worth taking a punt on them.'

'You haven't made many mistakes yet,' he said. 'If you think they're worth a try ...'

'But with plane tickets and hotels and all the rest it could cost us a lot if I'm wrong.'

'Follow your instincts,' Joe said, refusing to relieve me of the responsibility for my own decisions.

Taking a deep breath, I offered the group £200 a night and all their expenses, an offer they were happy to accept. I guess the chance to visit the homeland of The Beatles, and get paid for it, was pretty good, as well as the opportunity to build their international fan base. Now I just had to pray that Derek was right about the record they were planning to release.

When I got back to the UK I set about building a tour around them, not able to risk making them the only big name on the posters. I put them on the same bill as Unit 4 + 2, who were about to have a number one hit with 'Concrete and Clay' after Kenny Everett championed them on pirate radio, and with a group called Them, which was where Van Morrison started, and various other acts.

The Musicians' Union initially protested about us bringing an American act over, claiming they were taking work from our own musicians, but a deal was done for the Dave Clark Five (a group who had knocked The Beatles off the number one position with their first hit, 'Glad All Over') to go to America in exchange and everyone was happy.

By the time The Byrds arrived in England in 1965 Derek's prediction had come true. Their version of Bob Dylan's 'Mr Tambourine Man' had been released, just two weeks after Bob's own version, and was sitting comfortably at number one.

I'd put a lot of money and effort into this tour and I was determined to fill every theatre, keeping up the momentum of their record's success. I had posters printed up, saying 'The Byrds is Coming', aping the campaign for Hitchcock's film *The Birds*, which had come out shortly before. I used to do big poster campaigns for all my tours. Some of the sites would be bought on places like the underground and on railway stations, but I would also hire fly-posters to spread them wherever they could before a gig. Fly-posting was a good, cheap way of getting the word out on to the street, although there could be problems with the authorities and fights used to break out between rival fly-posters as they competed over the best sites. Advertising in the music business was still very old fashion compared with the sort of thing that happens today. The ads looked pretty much the same as they had before the war. We used to use a printer in Manchester and their rep used to come down to see us in a suit and tie, carrying a briefcase. Around 1970 everything changed in the advertising and promotion world and it all became much more creative, run by people with long hair and jeans. It was like walking into a completely new world, as people like the Saatchi brothers took over the business.

Grand Metropolitan had opened a brand new hotel, the Europa, in the street running from Grosvenor Square to Oxford Street (it is now a member of the Marriott Group), and they had been asking us to put some stars in their rooms, so I booked The Byrds in there. Some members of the group were heavily into drugs (being from California, where the whole 'summer of love' thing really kicked off a couple of years later), psychedelia and all the rest, which made the hotel management very jumpy. The chambermaids couldn't understand what the group was doing with the towels – they were laying them along the bottom of the doors to stop the smell of the marijuana escaping into the corridors.

Despite the fact that experimenting with drugs was becoming very fashionable (it would be a couple of years before The Beatles released Sgt Pepper and Mick Jagger was notoriously arrested at Keith Richards' house in a high-profile drug bust), I always made it a golden rule not to get involved with that side of the business. But I can't pretend now that I didn't know that it was going on with a lot of the performers and their entourages, even though I pretended not to notice at the time. If you are trying to build a successful business you have to make sure you aren't breaking any laws or the whole thing can come tumbling down around your ears. Rumours and mythologies about drug use might enhance the reputations of performers, reinforcing their hippie images, but for a businessman like me it would just have been a criminal stigma.

The group came out with their next hit, 'All I Really Want to Do', while they were on the tour and it became the fastest-selling single CBS had ever had over here. This was despite the fact that Cher brought out the same song at the same time and inevitably grabbed a chunk of the sales. As an exotic married couple, Sonny and Cher were a global phenomenon at the time, having just released 'I Got You Babe'.

When The Byrds were awarded a platinum disc for 'Mr Tambourine Man' they very kindly gave it to me to show their appreciation for the way I backed them at the beginning and I still have it on my wall amongst my other trophies. Gestures like that mean a lot, maybe even more than the people realize at the time they make them, especially when you get to the end of your career and start to look back at the high points. No one in the business resents the amount of recognition and adoration that is accorded to performers, partly because it is always good for business, but it is occasionally nice to have it acknowledged that there are other people working just as hard behind the scenes to bring the musicians and the fans together.

While I was in LA I also booked a singer called Nancy Wilson, who was big at the time with a Grammy-winning album and her own television show, and I teamed her up with the Ted Heath Orchestra for a tour in England in 1965, the same year as The Byrds. Looking back through my books I see I was paying Nancy £2,800 a night, which shows she was a big star, since I was only paying Ted Heath £950 a night for his whole orchestra.

It was always a gamble, deciding who would be able to draw in the crowds and who would prove to be too expensive. I did a tour with my cousins, Mike and Bernie, that year too and lost a lot of money. They were very big names by then but the audiences just didn't turn up for a live show. Maybe it was because they could see them for free on television without leaving the comfort of their own homes, or maybe it was because Mike and Bernie weren't using enough good new material. Television could be a problem for comedy acts

83

because material that they could keep using and re-using in live venues in front of new audiences could be used up in one go in a big television show seen by millions. The old-style variety bill just didn't pull people into the theatres in the way it had before television arrived. Now it was the rock and pop music tours that were really working well, with names like The Walker Brothers, Chris Farlowe, The Small Faces, Spencer Davis, The Kinks and virtually everyone who had a hit record at the time and wanted to cash in on their success and perform live for their fans. Unlike today, where a lot of stars are made by producers and technicians in the studios, backed by carefully made videos, almost every performer in the sixties could stand up and do a live show because that was the only way for them to get started. They would build a local following in pubs and clubs around their own areas first so that by the time they got to London and started to try and crack the national and international markets they were already experienced and professional (even if old-timers like Joe didn't think so!).

The Walker Brothers were a huge American act in the sixties and seventies with gigantic hits like 'Make It Easy on Yourself' and 'The Sun Ain't Gonna Shine Anymore'. They weren't actually brothers (just as the Kaye Sisters weren't real sisters), being three musicians who formed a band in 1964. Gary Walker (real surname Leeds) was on drums. Scott Walker (real surname Engel) was a bass player and had played in a band behind PJ Proby and had the idea of following PJ's example of trying to break into the British pop scene. John Walker (real name Maus) was lead singer on their first record, 'Pretty Girls Everywhere', but it didn't do that well. When Scott took over lead vocals on 'Make It Easy on Yourself' it sold a million copies around the world and the group became a serious rival to The Beatles in the eyes of their fans. The pressures of success and arguments within the group proved too much for Scott, however, who became depressed and eventually disappeared into a monastery.

After the group had split John asked me to manage his solo career. He was a good-looking guy and he could sing, but he wasn't hugely talented. Like The Everly Brothers, they should have stayed together, because that was how the magic had happened. He was a very nice man, maybe too nice for the pop business, but he had a girlfriend who was always interfering, which is a nightmare for managers. I tried to persuade him to find someone else to sing with him to support his voice, but the girlfriend kept saying John had to do his own thing. This was a period when there were a lot of drugs around on the pop scene and a lot of artists were hard to talk to and reason with, partly because they were a bit spaced out and partly because they tended to believe their own publicity and think they are invincible. Looking back now I think perhaps I should have pushed him more towards films and away from music. We made an album and sold a lot of copies in Japan, where The Walker Brothers had done their final tour before breaking up. In fact, I re-licensed that album to the Japanese recently, forty years after the Walker Brothers disbanded.

Whenever I had to go to the shows and meet the stars I would often take a girlfriend with me. In 1966 I was due to take one girl to a concert at a time when I fell for someone else and decided to take her instead. I told the first girl that I wasn't going to be going after all, assuming she would just stay at home. When I got to the Odeon in Blackpool, however, and went round to The Small Faces' dressing room to introduce my new girlfriend, I found the other one already there, sitting on Ronnie Wood's lap, having got the train upon her own. (Ronnie later became rock royalty, of course, as one of The Rolling Stones.)

There were a lot of business people who were seeing the same potential in rock and roll that I was. The Small Faces were handled by Don Arden, Sharon Osbourne's father, as were Wizzard, ELO, Lynsey de Paul and Ozzy Osbourne himself. A lot of people found Don difficult, and since finding fame herself Sharon has written a whole book on the subject, but I always got on well with him. The family lived just down the road from us when we moved to Wimbledon and Sharon was a frumpy little thing in those days, before she underwent her transformation in a media diva. Don seemed to be a good father, to me.

I first met him when he was an actor and singer and he used to appear in pantomimes for Joe for £40 a week, before he decided there would be more money to be made from working behind the scenes managing other people. He used to play Abanaza, the villain in Aladdin, and went on playing the same character in real life from then on, giving people the impression he was some sort of gangster if they didn't know any better. I took no notice of all his nonsense, having known plenty of real hard men when I was growing up, and maybe that was why we always got on well: that and the fact that we were both in the same business and both from similar backgrounds.

At one time I was managing Carl Perkins, an American artist who wrote 'Blue Suede Shoes', the big Elvis hit. I got a man called Felton Jarvis, Elvis's producer, to do an album with Carl in Nashville, also called 'Blue Suede Shoes', which was the last album he made. Don Arden bought it from me and was supposed to be releasing it on his record label but for some reason it never happened. I dealt with him over other artists too, like Raymond Froggatt.

Slim Whitman was another artist I had a long relationship with early on in my career, giving me an insight into the potential of the country stars, who did not receive nearly as much publicity in Europe as rock and pop stars but still had big, loyal followings and sold a lot of records and theatre seats. I first toured with Slim in 1968, and our last tour together was in 2004, nearly forty years later. He had a lot of hits in Britain and there were times when he was more popular over here than he was in America, although Michael Jackson later named him as one of his ten favourite vocalists. As far back as 1955 Slim had a hit with 'Rose Marie', which was the longest-running number one ever in the UK (eleven weeks) until Bryan Adams broke the record thirty-seven years later in 1992 with 'Everything I Do, I Do It For You', which stayed at number one for sixteen weeks when it was featured in a big-budget Robin Hood film starring Kevin Costner. Not even The Beatles or Englebert

Humperdinck's 'Release Me' managed to topple Slim's record in the sixties.

Slim was a wonderful client and always completely loyal to me. If any other promoter approached him with an offer or a suggestion he would always refer them to me, even if they were offering him more money. That sort of loyalty is a rare thing in the music business, although I was lucky enough to meet a few people of that calibre in the coming years, as well as the many insecure, over-sensitive and plain treacherous ones.

Proclamation

WHEREAS, MERVYN CONN HAS GAINED INTERNATIONAL RECOGNITION AS A RECORD PRODUCER AND AS A PROMOTER OF RECORDING EVENTS AND CONCERTS; AND

WHEREAS, MERVYN CONN, THROUGH HIS EXPERTISE IN STAGING CONCERTS IN NUMEROUS COUNTRIES THROUGHOUT THE WORLD, ORIGINATED THE INTERNATIONAL FESTIVAL OF COUNTRY MUSIC TEN YEARS AGO; AND

WHEREAS, THIS ANNUAL FESTIVAL AT WEMBLEY, ENGLAND HAS BECOME THE LARGEST SINGLE EVENT IN EUROPE AND IS BEING EXPANDED TO FESTIVALS IN SWEDEN AND AND FINLAND; AND

WHEREAS, THROUGH HIS CONTINUING EFFORTS AND REPUTATION AS ONE OF EUROPE'S LEADING MUSIC PERFORMERS, MERVYN CONN ESTABLISHED POPULARITY OF COUNTRY MUSIC IN ENGLAND AND AIDED CAREERS OF THE GREATEST COUNTRY MUSIC ENTERTAINERS IN COUNTRY MUSIC.

NOW, THEREFORE, I, RICHARD FULTON, MAYOR OF NASHVILLE, DO HEREBY PROCLAIM APRIL 9, 1983 AS

Mervyn Conn Day

AND TO EXPRESS OUR APPRECIATION FOR HIS OUTSTANDING EFFORTS IN BEHALF OF COUNTRY MUSIC.

IN WITNESS WHEREOF, I HAVE HEREUNTO SET MY HAND ON THIS, THE EIGHTH DAY OF APRIL, 1983.

Richard Fulton
Mayor

★ Mervyn Conn Day Proclamation ★

★ First Wembley Festival ★

★ Laura and me, 1970 ★

★ Lily and me, 1946 ★

★ Sarah Vaughan, Billy Eckstine and me, 1986 ★

★ Princess Anne and me, 1988 ★

★ Me in 1972 ★

★ Johnny Cash and June Carter, 1966 ★

★ *Patrick Duffy (from Dallas) and me at Wembley, 1987* ★

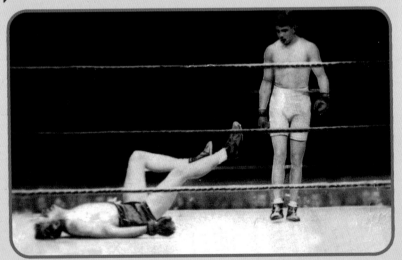

★ *My uncle Jack Bloomfield, knocking out Bomber Billy Wells, 1924* ★

Dolly Parton, George Hamilton IV
and me at Wembley, 1979 ★

★ Prince Edward and me, 1988 ★

★ Laura and me with President Jimmy Carter at the White House, 1984 ★

Pete Murray, Marlene Dietrich
and me ★

★ Audience at Wembley ★

★ Tammy Wynette ★

★ Me and Wally Whyton ★

★ Buck Owens ★

★ Boxcar Willie ★

★ Lily ★

Left to right: Jerry Lee Lewis, Murray Cash, Steve Gotley (MD Polygram Records) and me

Waylon Jennings

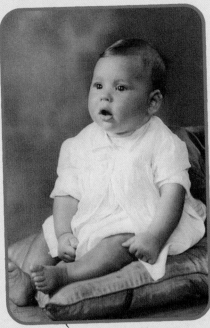

Me in 1935

Me circa 1948

★ Lily and me in Belgium ★

★ Me in Portugal ★

★ Me age six ★

★ Me and Laura ★

★ Me at Gerrard Street Club ★

★ Lily, Dad and me at my bar mitzvah ★

★ Left to right: Oliver, Joseph, Scarlett and Charity ★

★ Left to right: Rolf Harris and his wife, Frank Ifield, Olivia Newton John,
Slim Whitman, Mickey and Griff, George Hamilton IV and me ★

★ Emmylou Harris ★

★ Willie Nelson ★

★ Dad and me ★

★ Dad ★

★ Lily and me ★

★ Oliver and Scarlett ★

★ Lily and Sophia (my great granddaughter) ★

★ Me in Dad's taxi ★

★ Lily and Dad ★

★ Me modelling my own designs ★

★ Margaret Thatcher, Laura and me ★

★ Me with my youngest daughter Lily and granddaughter Kitty ★

★ Iris, Jacob, Rachael and Mick ★

★ Lily ★

★ Me with my great friend Jimmy Tarbuck ★

★ Me with Lily ★

★ Me with Mike and Bernie Winters ★

★ Me with Joan Collins and Christopher Biggins ★

★ Me today, ★
Photo taken by Jessica Dobbs

★ The Riviera Club, where I lost all my money ★

★ Phil Swern and me ★

★ My engagement to Shan Kaye of the Kaye Sisters at the Hilton Hotel ★

★ My marriage to Laura, 1969 ★

★ Beatles Christmas Show Poster ★

The Beatles, Cilla Black, Rolf Harris and Billy J Kramer.
★ *Rehearsals of The Beatles Christmas Show at Finsbury Park Astoria, 1963* ★

★ *A selection of posters* ★

★ Johnny ★ Cash ★

While I was in LA Queen Elizabeth was doing a royal tour of Canada and the Canadians put on a Royal Command Performance for her in Toronto along the lines of the annual Royal Variety Show in London. I was sitting by the hotel pool reading a report of the show in the *LA Times* and noticed that they were talking about a group who had appeared on the bill. The journalist was saying they were 'the new Beatles', which definitely caught my attention. Everyone at that time was always looking for 'the new Beatles' since the group had become the biggest showbusiness phenomenon in the world, even bigger than Elvis or Sinatra.

I flew up to Toronto the following day to see if I could find them. (These days, of course, I would have been able to bring them up on YouTube without moving away from the hotel pool.) The act was a group called The Travellers and, when I got to see them perform, were very good, but a bit too folksy for my taste, and certainly nothing like The Beatles. The trip, however, wasn't wasted because they put me into the Four Seasons Hotel, which led to me being asked to do a radio interview by the hotel's public relations people. A few hours after the interview was broadcast a Canadian called Saul Holiff rang my hotel room. He had heard the broadcast and had an idea of his own.

'I manage a singer called Johnny Cash,' he said. 'Would you be interested in bringing him to England?'

I'd vaguely heard the name and I agreed to meet Saul, who turned out to be a lovely man. He had been born in London to Russian parents and was running a drive-in restaurant where touring rock and roll bands used to hold autograph-signing sessions. Johnny had asked Saul to be his manager after one of these sessions and legend has it they signed a contract there and then on a single sheet of yellow paper. I did a bit of research and found that Johnny was doing pretty well in America with Sun Records, despite having been overshadowed first by Elvis and then by Jerry Lee Lewis. He had had an enormous hit with 'Ring of Fire' and had been touring with the Carter family after an introduction from Saul. They were a very well-established family act in the country music world, and Johnny had fallen in love with June Carter. He had also already developed problems with drink and drugs, becoming addicted at one stage to amphetamines.

I agreed to take him on tour in England, paying about $1,500 a night for him, June and all his musicians. It doesn't sound like much now, but you have to remember that the most expensive seats in the house would only have cost a guinea (£1.05 to those too young to remember). It does show, however, that Johnny was still not as famous as he soon would be, since I was paying so much more than that for an act like Nancy Wilson.

By the time the tour dates came round and Johnny and June boarded the plane for England I had bought myself an Aston Martin. I proudly drove my new toy out to meet them from the airport, not thinking about how I was going to have to squash poor June into the tiny back seat. It was the first time I had met either of them but we got on instantly and were destined to become good friends over the years. The stalwart June made no protest about the cramped car seat as we sped back into central London.

I had booked them into the Rubens Hotel behind Buckingham Palace. When we arrived Johnny tipped the porter £5 for bringing his bags up to the room and I had to explain that that wasn't how things were done in Britain – half a crown or a ten bob note would be more than enough. Johnny was still in the middle of getting a divorce from his first wife, Vivian, and he couldn't even share a hotel room with June in case Vivian's lawyers got to hear of it. When I found out his personal predicament and realized how much he and June wanted to be together I suggested that they should borrow my flat in Canonbury for as long as they were in England and they happily accepted the offer. Although it was a great flat it did have some drawbacks, such as not having a washing machine (such luxuries did not come as standard in those days). I suggested that rather than spend hours in a public laundromat, they should take any dirty washing to my mother's flat. I had already taken them round there for the Sabbath dinner and Johnny had managed to charm my parents completely. I knew Mum would be delighted, as she always wanted to be involved in my life in any way possible, and she loved mixing with showbusiness stars and characters as much as I did. She and June spent a lot of time together as result, chatting all the time. One day, while ironing Johnny's trousers, June found $40 in the pocket.

'Look what I just found, Lil,' she said, holding up the money.

'Keep it, don't tell him,' Mum advised without missing a beat. 'He'll never notice.'

As Johnny was still largely unknown outside America it was a hard sell to fill the theatres some nights. In some venues like Liverpool, however, he was sold out mainly because of all the Irish people living in the city. He'd written a song called 'Forty Shades of Green' in 1961 about Ireland, which they loved, but he hadn't had any big hits in Britain by that stage.

Despite the fact that the Aston Martin had virtually no room in the back, Johnny always wanted to travel around the country with me rather than having a more spacious car and a driver. I was happy to chauffeur him because I liked him so much, but poor old June would be forced to spend hours crammed into the back with her knees up under her chin, while Johnny sat beside me in the passenger seat, talking and talking and talking as we ate up the miles between the venues. I guess she was so in love with him she would have been willing to put up with virtually any discomfort as long as it kept him happy. He talked about his difficult childhood, about working in the cotton fields when

91

he was just five years old, surviving the Depression, joining the Air Force, his first marriage and his children. He had been badly affected by the death of his older brother, Jack, who had been pulled into a mechanical saw in a mill where he was working and cut almost in two. He had lived for a week after that, in terrible pain, and Johnny felt deeply guilty about the whole incident because he said he'd had a premonition on the morning of the accident. Their mother had experienced the same thing and had tried to persuade Jack to go fishing with Johnny instead of going to work but Jack had refused, saying the family needed the money too much.

Because Johnny had been in the American Air Force he wanted to play theatres on American military bases on the days when we didn't have other venues booked. Michael Black (Don Black's brother) was booking airbases at the time so I made all those arrangements through him. There was an American officers' club in the Bayswater Road called the Columbia Club, which we played, and several other bases around the country. Quite a few of the American stars wanted to play these venues, particularly the smaller country acts, so Michael and I were often able to work together during those years.

Country music was beginning to attract the attention of musicians in other areas. Elvis Costello had made his name as a punk rock singer with his band, The Attractions. He was a good friend of Nick Lowe, who was married to June Carter's daughter, Carlene, and the two of them sang at several of my events, which later led to Elvis having a huge hit with a George Jones song, 'Good Year for the Roses', and releasing a country album.

George Jones was a big star in his own right, but was also married to Tammy Wynette, and the first time they came over to perform together at the festival in 1974 was a country milestone. They shared her manager, however: George Ritchie. I had them booked for a tour together a few years later and they were due to come over to Europe with Ritchie, all good friends together. Just before the tour happened the marriage broke up and the tour had to be cancelled. Tammy then went on to marry Ritchie and I did other tours with George later.

Before Johnny Cash arrived I had recently done a tour with Roy Orbison, who I then discovered lived just across the road from Johnny, although I didn't know it at the time. Roy's shows had been packed out every night because of the string of hits he had already had, like 'Only the Lonely,' 'Crying' and 'Pretty Woman'. Ironically it had originally been Johnny who had recommended that Roy should go and see Sam Phillips at Sun Records when the two singers met while playing on a local radio station. At that stage Roy was part of a band called Teen Kings. He was a very talented man, but a strange character, very different from most of the artists I dealt with, very quiet and shy. He wouldn't have said boo to a goose and he was a real perfectionist when it came to the music.

Although I liked Johnny enormously, his moods could sometimes be unpredictable. I was on tour in Germany with him and Carl Perkins one time when a hotel receptionist said something that annoyed them. The two of them went out to the shops, bought two cans of black paint and re-decorated the hotel room. Guess who got given the bill for that little rock-and-roll moment?

Another time he'd had a fight with June over something just before a show and he wouldn't come out of his room. Everyone had been up to have a go at coaxing him out with no success and eventually I went up myself and knocked on the door.

'John, it's Mervyn here.'

There was an angry snarl from the other side of the locked door.

'Come on, John,' I persevered, 'we've got to get the show on the road now.'

More growling and then the lock clicked and he emerged with a wry smile.

After the second tour we did together, when the rest of the group had flown back to America, Johnny, June and I went to Israel together on holiday and he paid for everything. Johnny was a genuinely religious man and because he was not a

93

household name in the Middle East he was able to walk around the streets of Jerusalem without anyone recognizing him. A few years later, when his fame became global, he wouldn't have been able to get away with that. I had never been a particularly religious person, but the whole experience of being in a city steeped in so much history was deeply moving.

During our years as friends I arranged one of the biggest breaks in Johnny's life: setting up the Folsom Prison television show. Granada Television rang me to ask if he would be willing to do a show with them and they went to America to film him in action, giving a concert at the prison. His whole life changed after that and he became a major international star. In 1967 he was up for the Country Music Association Award and he invited me over to sit at his table for the ceremony. The following year he asked me to move to Nashville and manage him. It was a flattering offer and I'm sure it would have been fun, but I didn't want to live there full time and give up everything I had built up in Britain, losing my roots.

Johnny and I worked closely for many years until he finally changed managers. He was taken on by Lou Robin who was a promoter himself and didn't need my services any more in order to bring Johnny to the European market. I think there were other reasons why I lost touch for a while too.

I had once been out with a girl called Dee. She worked as a secretary in Don Black's office when I met her, and was going out with Bobby Butlin, the son of the famous holiday camp founder. She gave up Bobby Butlin for me and became very serious about our relationship, while I was still rushing around far too much to be able to commit to anything. One Sunday she arranged to cook lunch for me at her flat. I had Nancy Wilson on tour at the time and that evening Nancy was due to perform at the Odeon, Hammersmith with Ted Heath's orchestra. Rehearsals dragged on and I didn't get to Dee's place until about five in the afternoon, by which time she was really furious about the ruined meal. This was all long before the invention of the mobile phone so people tended not to keep one another constantly updated about any changes to their plans as they are able to do now. The argument went on and on and eventually I walked out, ending the relationship. She later went out with a man called Alan Tinkner who was a partner with Lou Robin in Johnny's new management company. Although I never knew for sure if there was a connection, they didn't seem to want to have me around for a few years after that.

I didn't tour with Johnny again until the eighties, by which time I was running a string of country festivals all the way across Europe and had many more fingers in many more pies.

Many years later, after he had passed away, I wrote a musical called *My Friend, Johnny Cash*, which I wanted to stage in the West End. The storyline was about us putting on a show together and it contained all the big songs that he was so famous for, so I needed the permission of his estate, which by that time was being run by his son. They didn't give permission because they were about to stage another show on Broadway and the movie, *Walk the Line*, was out, with Joaquin Phoenix playing Johnny and Reese Witherspoon playing June. The film was nominated for five Oscars, and Reese won the Best Actress award.

Establishing The Festival

Joe decided to cut down on his workload and leave the office in 1967. He planned to work from home, still looking after some of his favourite acts, including Mike and Bernie. He asked me what I wanted to do. I said I wanted to keep going and take over the lease on Chandos Place from him. I felt I could pull in enough business to make it work and I moved into Joe's office overlooking Coutts Bank, with a view down to Trafalgar Square, and I installed a sound system so I could play my music, test records and listen to new talent.

Joe's wife Elsa, the mother of his first three children, had tragically died of cancer in 1962, at the age of fifty-six. Joe had then met a young agent called Irene, who used to work with us in Chandos Place, and they had got married in 1967. Irene went on to have enormous success promoting the career of Roger Whittaker, who was famous for whistling on his records and had big hits with easy-listening titles like 'Durham Town' and 'New World in the Morning'. Irene also had a fourth child for Joe, a little girl they called Natasha. Natasha was another reason why Joe decided to work from home, as he wanted to play a big part in her life, something he probably felt he had missed out on with the other children because he had been so busy building the agency and making a name for himself in the business. Now that I've got a new baby later in life myself I can completely understand how he must have felt, knowing that the time I am going to be here with her is bound to be limited.

By that stage Joe had taught me well. I was experienced at handling the tours for country stars like Johnny Cash and Slim Whitman, as well as for the pop singers and rock and rollers. I was hiring road managers to do a lot of the slogging around and I was ready to be sole captain of my own ship. In the beginning I had always been the one out on the road with the acts while Joe had been back at the office, so I knew the business from the bottom up. I had served my apprenticeship.

Moss Empires owned the building in Chandos Place and I became their lessee. I rented the top floor out to someone else to help with the overheads. I had one secretary and a couple of guys: Mike Stone, an American who was managing a girl and doing something with Columbia Films, and Cyril Smith, who was working with me on managing a group called The Peddlers and who was a manager of a place called The Pickwick Club, which was where I first saw The Peddlers playing and which I often used for events like the first reception I ever held for Johnny Cash when he arrived in England.

My budding empire was all a patchwork of deals and partnerships put together to generate the revenue I needed to keep everything going. I had an internal accountant called Ken Salter, who was with me for years and protected my resources fiercely. Getting money out of him was like getting blood out of a stone, which was very useful with so many artists around, all of whom were always hard up and asking for more. I don't think he and I ever had a cross word in all the years we worked together.

I had also started my own record company. I started with a production deal with CBS Records, recording and managing acts like Donnie Albert. Donnie had a record called 'Get Ready', but he didn't think that CBS was doing enough to promote it and he turned up at my office to complain – not that there was anything I could do about it. He had a cigarette, which he waved before my eyes, as I pushed it away he smashed me in the face, pulled out a gun and threatened to shoot me. He had managed to smash the whole office before the police arrived and sorted him out. I think he was sent back to America.

I went on to get my own label, Carnaby Records, with Pye doing the distribution. I managed The Peddlers, who were brilliant and the epitome of cool, James Royal, who had a huge hit song in Europe called 'Call My Name', which was a very French-sounding record, and several others. I used to go down to Cannes each year to Midem, the industry festival, which was launched in 1967 and grew to become the biggest in the world, and I had a music publishing company to handle the songs that my artists had written, bringing in an expert to deal with all the administration.

I was James's manager as well, so when CBS in France arranged a big promotional trip for him I went along too. In Paris they put us into the George V Hotel and it felt like we had arrived on top of the world. Taking full advantage of the record company's generosity we ran up the sort of horrendous bill that I would later have other artists running up at my expense, so I'm not surprised that the record company went through the roof when they realized we'd been running open food and drink and telephone bills for anyone who cared to come to the hotel and party with us, filling the room with girls and drinking champagne like it was water.

We went on to tour clubs all over the country with James's group, which was very exciting, staying in nice hotels and collecting the money from each of the clubs. We tempered our behaviour after the Paris fling, wanting to do a good job of launching the act. The record company spent a good bit of money on him but for some reason James never crossed the line in Britain in the same way as he did in places like France and Belgium, and to make it on the international scene then you really had to make it into the British or American charts. One of James's records was produced by Tony Hatch, who became a good friend. Tony produced Petula Clark's big hits and we became very friendly with her, her husband Claude and her manager John Ashby, who had gone out with my future wife long before I met her (he had also gone out with Judith Durham of The Seekers at the same time).

The Peddlers had similar difficulty breaking through into the mainstream, their records always hovering around at the bottom of the charts in Britain.

'Call my Name' was written by a Canadian man called Ralph Murphy who had travelled to England with a guy called Jim Clayson on the *QE II* liner, entertaining passengers to pay for their tickets. My mother happened to be on the same ship, coming back from a holiday in America with my father. She was impressed and pulled Ralph to the side one night and told him to come and see me when he got to London.

'My son's in the music business,' she told them proudly. 'He might be able to help you.'

'That's what we're coming to England for,' Ralph said. 'We'll definitely do that.'

They came to see me at the office with a tape of their material and told me they wanted to be song writers more than entertainers.

'That would suit me', I said, 'because I'd like to do some publishing. Why don't you write me some songs?'

'The trouble is,' Ralph admitted, 'we've got nowhere to stay.'

'I've got a flat in Canonbury. There's a spare bedroom there. You can do some writing and we'll sign a publishing deal.'

They happily agreed to the deal but they were so distracted by the excitements of the city that they never seemed to be staying in to do any writing.

'That's it,' I said eventually, when still no songs had been handed over. 'I'm locking you in.'

That was exactly what I did, and they came up with 'Call my Name', among others. Ralph then got a job at Mills Music, the music publishers in Tin Pan Alley (Denmark Street in Soho), who did all my publishing administration work for me, and went on to write for acts like Vanity Fair and Brotherhood of Man. He started going out with one of my old girlfriends, a girl called Anne, who also worked at Mills Music, and eventually married her. He worked his way up the company and then went to New York as their Director of Production and wrote more songs like the country hit 'Good Enough to Be Your Wife', sung by Jeannie C Riley. He teamed up with Roger Cook to form the Picalic Group and Pic-A-Lic Music

Publishing and had more than twenty number-one records, publishing 'Talking in Your Sleep' by Crystal Gayle. Pic-A-Lic became one of the most successful independent publishers in Nashville and eventually sold to EMI. Ralph, the penniless musician who arrived in my London office all those years ago, ended up joining ASCAP, one of the biggest music publishing administrators in the world, and he is now their chief man in Nashville.

There was another guy at Mills Music, working as a plugger, called Tony Hiller, who I became very friendly with. He eventually worked his way up to be second in charge of the company. He was also a writer and became very successful, winning the Eurovision Song Competition with Brotherhood of Man in 1976 with 'Save Your Kisses for Me' and wrote for a huge range of stars from Elton John to Olivia Newton John, The Osmonds to Crystal Gayle. Tony started out as part of a song and dance duo, The Hiller Brothers, appearing with all the stars of the time, like Alma Cogan, Matt Munro and Roger Whittaker. His song 'United We Stand' has been recorded by over a hundred different artists and we still do bits and pieces together today, mainly for charities.

I probably should have concentrated on building the publishing side of the business and looked for partners who could have helped me grow bigger, but I was having too good a time and I liked being in control of everything. At one stage my stockbrokers, James Capel, suggested that they could arrange for me to buy Boosey and Hawkes, who are the largest classical music publisher in the world. I turned them down, but looking back now I can see I should have taken their advice, because publishing is one of the most lucrative sides of the business and doesn't involve a great deal of work. Any money I would have had to borrow to do the deal would have been repaid many times over. At the time, however, I was so involved in so many things I didn't think I could handle such a major commitment. There were several times in my life when I know that I failed to make the jump to the next stage business-wise, and that was one of them.

I had fingers in every pie and although the record company was not a huge success in Britain I was able to sell quite a bit abroad because everything to do with British music was in great demand at that time. The Beatles had set the ball rolling but there had been many other successes following in their footsteps. I probably would have made more money in the long term if I had concentrated on the recording and publishing sides of the business, but my heart was more in the touring and the live shows and I was always on the lookout for ways to create something new from it.

I also kept a finger in the variety pie through Mike and Bernie. When a film of Batman was released someone wrote a comedy song 'That Man Batman' and brought it to me, asking if I thought Bernie would like to sing it. I took it to Bernie, who thought it was worth a go, dressing up as Batman for the publicity. That led to us doing a complete album of kids songs called 'Mike and Bernie in Toyland', which sold about 40,000 copies through outlets like Woolworths, who used to be the biggest record sellers in the country, mostly selling cut-price products. The guy who helped me to promote the record was Phil Swern. I had first met Phil in 1964 when he was about sixteen years old and worked as a record plugger for a slightly shady record company called Strike Records. He has gone on to become one of the most important radio producers and music collectors in the country. His collection includes every UK top forty hit since charts began in 1952 and he currently produces *Pick of the Pops* and *Sounds of the 60s* and used to produce the Bob Harris Show. He also devises the questions for the PopMaster quiz on Radio 2's Ken Bruce Show.

I noticed that when I was staging Johnny Cash's second tour, after his international career had really taken off and every show was sold out, I would get a lot of phone calls from wealthy individuals who wanted tickets and I was beginning to understand the growing world of corporate entertainment. One of these customers was a man called Charles Williams who owned a lot of pubs and was a director of Fuller, Smith and Turner, the brewers. He used to send cases of champagne to the office to make sure he got the best tickets and we duly became good friends.

'You must come to one of my pubs', he told me one day, 'to see some of the acts that we hire.'

To be honest, I wasn't that interested in seeing British country acts when I could get the real thing from America (I later changed my mind when I signed a guy called Raymond Froggatt, who was excellent and had a big hit with 'Red Balloon'), but in 1968 I took up the invitation and went to The Red Cow in Brentford. The acts actually weren't that bad, but Charles seemed to have other things on his mind.

'Don't worry about them,' he said when I murmured something polite about the music. 'I didn't actually bring you here to see them. I'm going to show you something amazing tonight.'

He took me outside to his car, refusing to tell me any more, and we headed into London to the Russell Hotel in Bloomsbury's Russell Square. He led the way towards the hotel's ballroom where there was a crowd of several hundred people gathered.

'Who have they come to see?' I asked, assuming he'd brought me to see an act he had an interest in. 'Who's on?'

'There's nobody on,' Charles said. 'They're forming the British Country Music Association. They've come here from all over the country.'

I was stunned to find that there was that level of interest in country music in Britain. I knew that I could fill theatres with big names like Johnny, but I hadn't realized there was this widespread an interest in the whole genre. It set me thinking as I drove home that night. I had probably been involved with country music for longer than anyone else in the London entertainment world. 'I know what I'll do,' I thought, 'I'll put a big event together, something that people like the ones I've just met in Russell Square would be keen to come to.' Getting to America was expensive and difficult in those days, and seeing one or two acts at a time on tour had only a limited appeal. So, what if I were to bring over dozens of them and get them all performing in the same place at the same time? I was pretty sure I would be able to convince the stars and their managers

103

that this could be their way of raising their profiles and selling many more records in Britain.

The first thing I needed to sort out, however, was where I would hold such an event. It had to be somewhere big enough to make the whole thing financially viable. I was doing at least a hundred and fifty shows a year by then so I knew I could get to talk to virtually any venue owner I wanted. I was also directing the *Melody Maker* Awards ceremony at Wembley Arena, so I decided to go and talk to the management there and see what sort of a deal I could put together.

Melody Maker (*MM*) was the oldest music paper in the country, aimed directly at the musicians rather than the fans, which was where the *New Musical Express* (*NME*) was so successful. I also knew the owner of the *NME*. His name was Maurice Kinn and he had bought the paper for £1,000 in 1952, when it was just fifteen minutes from going bust, and built it up into the country's most successful music paper. I was first introduced to him by Joe Collins and in 1966 I started advertising with him, taking a half page to promote Johnny Cash, which was an unusual amount of space in those days. He was always very supportive with editorial coverage of the events. Maurice was credited with being instrumental in helping Sinatra re-launch his career in the fifties. He was a mad Arsenal fan as well. I remember after he sold the magazine he turned up at the football ground in a huge limousine. He went on to do a number of other things, including running a flower shop in Mayfair and staging rock concerts for the *Daily Mirror*.

The *MM* was founded in 1926 and finally merged with the *NME* in 2000. In the seventies, however, it had enormous credibility and was sometimes selling as many as a quarter of a million copies a week, so it was a big deal to be involved with it.

Having thought through what my proposal was going to be, I went up to Wembley a few days later. There was an indoor tennis tournament on and I was in the VIP section with John Evans, the General Manager of the arena, and John Connolly, who was Managing Director of the whole Wembley complex. I had plenty of time and a nice relaxed atmosphere in which to float my latest idea.

'I want to put on a country music festival,' I told them as we sipped champagne and watched the games. 'And I'd like to do it here. You know I've been touring with artists like Johnny Cash and I think there's a great feeling for the music in this country, which I think should be linked to a specific event.'

'That's interesting,' they said, which was a better reaction than I had got from a lot of my friends, who were so dazzled by rock and roll they thought country was a dead art form. A lot of them had told me they thought I was mad to even consider getting involved in something they saw as corny and old fashioned.

'If you give me a deal here,' I told the two Johns. 'I promise I will never take the event away from you in the future if it becomes successful.'

I knew that an offer like that would appeal to them because venues always like to have some definite fixtures booked in each year, events that they know they can bank on whenever they do a bit of financial forecasting. They agreed in principle there and then and we shook on the deal. In those days it was quite normal to do a deal on a verbal promise because people tended to keep to their word: there weren't nearly as many lawyers involved in the business back then! It turned out to be one of the best decisions I could have made. There was a wonderful family atmosphere about Wembley in those days and my relationship with those two men and their management teams was fantastic. We never had a cross word in all the years we worked together.

Having got the venue lined up, I needed next to set my mind to where I was going to find the talent. It was crucial that I book some big names, people that the fans would be familiar with and would be willing to travel to Wembley to see. One of my distributors for Carnaby Records was CBS, who were one of the biggest labels for country music in the US. Everything was split into different charts in those days: country, R&B, pop and so on. I went to the head of A&R there, Derek Everett, and told him about my plans to stage a country festival.

'I need to know about the talent,' I said. 'What can you tell me?'

'You've got to go to Nashville, really,' he said. 'That's where it's all happening now.'

I knew that Johnny had moved to Nashville with June now that they were married, and I knew it was the home of the Grand Ole Opry, but I didn't know much more about it than that. The Grand Old Opry was a venue and radio show that treated country music with incredible reverence. Elvis had performed there as a teenager but his rock style did not go down well and the management had suggested he went back to Memphis and 'resumed his career as a truck driver'. (Luckily he didn't take their advice.) The Byrds were virtually the only modern-looking group (as in long haired) to play there after they had recruited country-rock pioneer Gram Parsons to their ranks, replacing David Crosby, who went on to form the incredibly successful Crosby, Stills, Nash and Young. They didn't fare much better with their 'new-fangled ideas' than Elvis had, having to put up with a lot of cat calls, heckling and abuse from the purist country audience. I decided that if I was going to get to the heart of the country music world I needed to find out more about Nashville and the way it worked, so I booked myself a ticket.

This was a very different town from London, New York and Los Angeles. It was a time when an unsophisticated middle America was still struggling against the idea of racial integration. It was the time when Martin Luther King was assassinated in Memphis and the civil rights movement was fighting its biggest battles all across the country. When I got into town they were still separating rest rooms for blacks and whites, sending black people through different entrances in restaurants and making them travel at the backs of buses. Remembering the lesson I had learned from plunging into the restaurant business without taking expert advice, I decided I was going to need someone to guide me round the Nashville scene. I knew a guy called Murray Kash, who was married to a performer I knew well called Libby Morris. I liked him a lot so I phoned him and he came to see me. I explained my concept of a country festival in London and asked for his help.

'I need to meet the right people,' I explained. 'If this idea works I will take you on full time.'

Murray agreed and in Nashville we hired a local lady called Emily Bradshaw who ran a public relations company and who was waiting for us with a limousine on the runway when we landed. By the time we got to our hotel there was a banner welcoming me by name to Nashville. It was complete bullshit, of course, but it felt good nonetheless. Emily introduced me to an agent and music publisher called Hubert Long, who completely saw the potential of my idea, understanding that breaking into the British market could be a stepping stone for artists towards conquering the rest of Europe. He could see that if I succeeded in my plan the potential earnings for his clients could be enormous. He was a founding board member of the enormously influential Country Music Association and he opened every door for me. When the festival was up and going in London I created a 'Hubert Long Award' in his honour to show my appreciation. I will never forget how instrumental he was in getting the festival established. Not many of the agents and managers were as far sighted as he was – in fact, a lot of them didn't seem to be aware that there was a world outside America at all.

At our tenth festival I gave the Hubert Long Award to Dolly Parton, who I had first met in Nashville and who had performed at the festival in the early seventies when she was only just starting to become a big star and was coming to Britain for the first time ever. She was the most charming and professional of stars, even when I had to ask her to get up at five in the morning to fly to Finland and then again a few days later to fly on to Switzerland.

A singer called Tompall Glaser was also on that tour and refused to go on one night because he thought he should either be closing the first half or the whole show, above Dolly or Don Williams. Nobody was going to agree to that and I told Kenny Rogers about the problem. Kenny went looking for Tompall, told him not to be so stupid and just get out on stage. Tompall had been a fantastic success at the second festival, his performance provoking such a loud and physical reaction from the crowd that it actually caused clouds of the dust to fall from the aging Wembley rafters. Another popular star of the time was Roy Acuff, who was a singer, fiddler and promoter.

Hubert Long controlled a lot of the biggest artists in Nashville and he persuaded some of them to come over for peanuts to the first festival, knowing that there would be spin-offs to be had from building fan bases in Europe, which would more than pay for any investment of their time they made at the beginning. It was a very far-sighted decision. Rock and roll was taking over the world and country artists were going to have to work long and hard to hold on to their share of the record-selling pie worldwide. Wesley Rose of music publisher Acuff-Rose (Roy Acuff was his partner) was another big name in the business who was helpful to me at the beginning.

I was nervous about relying completely on ticket sales for income, but to begin with I couldn't convince anyone to provide any sponsorship. Big business wasn't too used to the idea of sponsoring the arts at that time; most of their attention was focused on linking their names with big sporting events. I needed to find another way to hedge my bets.

I decided to set up booths all round the perimeter of the arena and to try to persuade record companies, booze companies, clothes companies and anyone else who would be interested in reaching country fans to rent them. That way I would be guaranteed some income regardless of how many tickets were sold. In the end I managed to sell off about forty of these sites in that first year. Initially I just asked for a couple of hundred pounds from each exhibitor but once it had taken off I was able to put the prices up to more realistic levels. RCA and MCA paid £1,000 each to have a presence there, which was valuable source of cash flow in an operation that was already proving expensive to set up.

One of my customers was a man called Vince Power, who would buy a stand to promote his new music venue, The Mean Fiddler, in Harlesden. Since it was just down the road from

108

Wembley a lot of my stars would go down to the venue and young artists on stage would suddenly find themselves playing to the likes of Johnny Cash, Albert Lee or Boxcar Willie.

I also got help from the record companies towards paying for their artists' airline tickets. I was doing anything I could to get the money rolling in quickly enough to meet the rising outgoings. I needed to set up a permanent office in Nashville, staffed by four or five people, to help get everyone organized to travel. Emily joined the staff permanently and stayed with me all the way through to the last show I did in 1991. It soon became obvious that some of the stars needed a lot of hand-holding. Many of them were terrible at sorting out even the most basic practical matters, like ensuring they had up-to-date passports, tickets and accommodation. It all had to be done for them if we wanted to be sure they would be in London when we needed them. A lot of them came from outside Nashville, like Kris Kristofferson, who lived in Los Angeles, and they all needed to be brought together to a central point like Atlanta so that my team could pick them up and bring them all over at once. That way I knew I had control of them, like a teacher transporting a giant party of unruly kids. If they had been finding their way across the Atlantic individually God knows where half of them would have ended up. The airlines were very helpful because they knew I would be buying a hundred for more tickets at a time. One of the biggest problems was working out who should be at the front of the plane, since they were all used to flying first class when someone else was paying the bills and most of them thought they were bigger stars than their fellow travellers, or at least their managers did. It was as tricky as trying to work out the billing on an all-star show.

I would arrange for a fleet of limousines to be waiting for them at the airport in England, usually collecting them off flights arriving at about six in the morning, to bring them to the hotels where they would have been pre-registered and could go straight up to bed. I always wanted them to get some sleep on arrival because I would be waking them up at about four o'clock in the afternoon to get them ready to go to a big banquet to welcome them to London. The banquet would often end up being for about five hundred people because I would invite all the record companies as well as my bigger exhibitors. Everyone likes to say they have had dinner with the stars. To begin with I had to pay for everything myself, but as we moved on and sponsors started to come on board I was able to pass a lot of the costs of the banquet on to them because they wanted to brand the event in any way they could in order to reach such an influential bunch of people.

Terry Wogan came to several of my banquets because he and his producers, Alan Boyd and the late Paul Walters, always played a lot of country music on their Radio Two show and did a lot to help promote us. Wally Whyton, on *Country Meets Folk*, Stan Laundon, Phil Lewis, who was head of BBC Outside Broadcasting, and the DJ Bob Harris have also done so much to promote country. There was also David Allan who had the only BBC network country radio show at the time, called *Country Style*, and who I asked to compère the first festival with Murray Kash. David did all of the television commentaries from the festival for the BBC. The music journalist Tony Byworth first came to Wembley as a fan in 1969, but during the seventies he started writing for a number of different publications as well as editing *Country Music People*. In the eighties he became a publicist, representing a number of the artists we booked, including Merle Haggard, Willie Nelson and the Osmond Brothers.

So often I had to call in favours from friends at the last minute to keep everything going. I once asked Stan Laundon, who I knew had a car, to give Lynn Anderson and her husband, Glenn Sutton, a lift back to their hotel in London. What I didn't realize was that Stan's car was an old Ford Anglia, that Stan had only been driving for three years and that he had no more idea of how to find his way around London than around the moon. Stan cheerfully set off in the direction he thought might be right and it wasn't till they started driving through fields of cows and sheep that Lynn and Glenn realized he had no idea where he was going and politely asked him to stop so they could get out and find a taxi back into the West End.

Most of all, of course, nothing would have been possible without the loyal support of all the country fans, who would turn up year after year and gave me the support I needed to turn this into a viable business over twenty-two years.

I always put everyone up in the best hotels, places like the Dorchester, Grosvenor House or the Hyde Park. The Royal Garden in Kensington was my favourite for a long time because they gave me such great deals. I needed a lot of rooms because it wasn't just the Americans who needed to be put up: there was also my administrative staff and my technical people. These days every venue has its own lighting and sound systems, but back then you had to set up your own. It meant we had to get into Wembley four days before the festival started in order to build the set and all the exhibition stalls. I had to have the best people for the job because there was no room for making mistakes, and if you want to keep the best people you have to pay them well and look after them.

During the seventies and eighties I would create a country music industry in Europe, where there had been virtually nothing before. Before that the image of country music was all about hillbillies sitting on bales of hay and straw hats and dungarees, and the music was completely overshadowed by rock and roll. Within a few years of starting I had turned this on its head and country became a massive industry as a result. In the first year we took around £7,000 in ticket sales, by the end it was more like £300,000 and that was just in the UK, never mind all the European countries, plus the advertising, the sponsorship and the exhibition stands that surrounded the events. For the industry as a whole the festival opened the floodgates for the artists to build whole new careers, touring individually and selling millions of records they would never otherwise have sold. I did a tour with a singer called Buck Owens soon after the first festival, taking him to several countries and playing the Palladium, which made him the first country star to perform there, apart from Slim Whitman.

I had some brilliant staff over the years, without whom none of this would have been possible. My PA, Jackie Boyle Thomas, was with me for fifteen years and never stopped working. Malcolm Anthony was my company manager and Tony Erdman my head of security and personal bodyguard. Carl Lewis was my head booker and Will Norton was in charge of all the staging and sound. Warren Davies and Tony Barrow were the press officers who made sure the world knew about what was going on, and Ken Salter kept track of the money.

It was always a highly pressured time for me and I had to carry some heavy insurance with so many things that could potentially go wrong. The biggest insurance claim I had to make in all those years, however, was when Kris Kristofferson had to pull out at the last moment in the third year after his daughter was involved in a serious motorbike accident in California. He had been one of the headliners for the festival in England and Europe that year, and I had also arranged tour dates for him. A lot of people had to be refunded their ticket money after that. I had a young insurance broker called Willie Robertson, of Robertson Taylor at the time, who grew to be one of the biggest in the country. Willie was a real character, a flamboyant old Harrovian, who managed to handle the whole thing expertly. Thankfully Kris's daughter recovered and the insurance company paid up about £65,000, which was a substantial amount of money at the time. The only other large claim was when Tammy Wynette had a breakdown while she was over here and had to go home.

My relationship with the management at Wembley was always great, until Jarvis Astaire came on board. Jarvis was another man to emerge from the world of boxing, having started out staging bouts as a teenager during the war, going on to become a manager and part of Frank Bruno's promotional team, being responsible for bringing Muhammad Ali to England to defend his world title against Henry Cooper in 1966. He became Deputy Chairman of Wembley after I had been staging the festivals for a few years when the venue had money troubles and Jarvis offered to put in £1 million of his own money. His first wife had been an heiress of the Mappin and Webb jewellery fortune. After the first year had gone well I used to do a deal with Wembley for three years at a time, building up the number of days each year. As long as John Connolly and John Evans were there I had never had even a moment's problem – they had been such honourable and pleasant people to do business with. Jarvis and I did not get on in the same way, but we had known each other for years because of our family connections with boxing and because Micky Duff, who was a close associate of Jarvis's as a successful boxing promoter, had run an outworking factory in Shoreditch at the time when I was in the fashion business. Jarvis and I had also crossed paths at the Variety Club.

Because the setting up of the festival was so complex I used to call a meeting a couple of months beforehand for everyone who was involved, including the television people, exhibitors, radio and sound people, the set designers and builders, merchandisers, technicians, council officials and staff from Wembley itself. In the end there were fifty or more people coming to these meetings. I would be in the chair with a couple of secretaries, starting at ten in the morning and going on till lunchtime. In the middle of one of these meetings the door burst open and Jarvis strode in, flanked by a couple of his people.

'You can stop all this now,' he shouted. 'This won't happen because I've got a boxing match on the Thursday so you won't be able to do any setting up till that's over.'

I told him that this wasn't the right moment for us to be having this discussion and after the meeting I went straight to see the Chairman. In the end Jarvis got his way and it cost us a fortune to fit round him because we had to work through the night, so our relations became even more strained. When my lease needed to be renewed I was in a meeting with the management in what should have been little more than a 'rubber stamping', as they wanted the festival there as much as I wanted to stage it. Once again Jarvis barged into the room uninvited.

'You take this lot for a load of schmucks,' he said, 'don't you, Mervyn?'

'No,' I said, determined not to let him wind me up. 'Why should I do that?'

'You've got away with murder here for years, haven't you?'

'I don't think so, Jarvis. I think Wembley has been very satisfied with our association. It's been going for sixteen years now.'

'You remind me of me when I used to run the boxing at York Baths at your age,' he went on, obviously enjoying himself. 'I used to get deals down there with them and you're doing the same with these guys. We don't get anything out of your sponsorship deals.'

'Why should you?'

'It's going to change.'

'I'll tell you what,' I said. 'I've had enough of your rudeness, Jarvis. I'll take the festival somewhere else.'

With that I stormed out of the room, followed by the management, all assuring me that they didn't want me to go, trying to calm me down and eventually succeeding. The next time I saw Jarvis I had Roberta Flack singing in the conference centre and it was completely sold out.

'You've had it off here, son, haven't you?' he said cheerfully. 'Can't find a seat.'

'Well, you could buy one Jarvis,' I said.

Once the banquet was over each year we then had to concentrate on making sure the acts got to the stage when they were supposed to, and were totally happy. There would be eight acts appearing at the festival each day, so we would have to make sure they were got out of bed in time (never that easy with musicians), and then we would have to arrange for them to be shown round London and entertained during the hours when they weren't needed at Wembley. They would also need to be given whatever rehearsal and sound check times they needed. I would hire around twenty-five of the prettiest young girls I could find to direct and organize them once they were in the country. I always got young girls to do those sorts of jobs because I knew that even big stars found it harder to be rude to them, especially American men who, on the whole, I have found to have very good manners towards women.

I was constantly aware that in order to entice punters to a festival you have to offer them plenty to do. Most people, even

114

if they are avid fans, will not be willing to spend several days doing nothing but watching acts performing on stage. I couldn't expect them to just wander around the exhibition stands all day, however much the exhibitors might have liked that. People needed to feel involved in the whole event. To that end I hired the conference centre next to the Arena and ran a competition titled 'The Best of British Country', which would be the culmination of talent shows I had organized all round the country during the previous year, looking for undiscovered British acts, the sort of people who were performing in pubs and clubs, hoping one day for a big break. It was a bit like the *X Factor* heats that Simon Cowell runs now.

I would bring the twenty best acts to the conference centre and they would perform in front of a panel, which would consist of record company people, agents and star guests from America. The competition would run from ten in the morning up till three o'clock in the afternoon and was designed to keep people occupied until the main festival acts started. As the stars finished their rehearsals they would be brought over to the conference centre where they would be interviewed for BBC Radio in front of an audience, which gave people something else to watch, making them feel part of what was going on. At the same time I would have caterers giving private lunches for people who were important to the festival. During the evenings I would host more hospitality events where people could watch the show while they ate dinner. The whole thing was run like a giant military operation. I hired my Uncle Mick – the one who lived with Mum and Dad – as a host since he had worked all those years in the pub trade and had the gift of the gab. He helped with the corporate entertaining because he was such a nice guy and everyone always liked him.

The first year's lineup on 5 April 1969 included Loretta Lynn, Conway Twitty and George Hamilton IV. I had been particularly friendly with George ever since he first toured for me. The two of us have never exchanged a cross word or even felt the need to bother with a written contract in the forty or more years that we have been working together. Neither of us has ever doubted the other's word on anything, which I guess is why we have remained such good friends. Loretta also became a good friend from the first moment they arrived and I met them on the tarmac at Heathrow.

Not all the artists came from America. We also had a number of great acts from other countries like Ireland. I put a number of shows on in Ireland during the years of the troubles, but we never had any problems since the acts were all American. Catholics and Protestants seemed to be happy to mingle at my events. We always used to stay at the Europa Hotel outside Belfast but it got blown up and we had to look for another.

A young Irish promoter called Carmel Mannion tormented me for years about putting on a singer called Daniel O'Donnell. When she eventually secured him a spot on Terry Wogan's show I agreed to give him a chance. Despite the strict schedule he over ran and over ran, because the audience kept shouting for more. Finally the stage manager crawled out on to the stage to pull the mains plug. Daniel went on to become one of the biggest selling artists in the world.

Eight and a half thousand people showed up for the first festival (the venue could have taken eleven thousand so we could have squeezed a few more in but it was still a massive crowd), and the event lasted for six hours on stage, becoming the prototype for all the thousands of festivals that have happened around the world since then, from Glastonbury, which started a couple of years later, to Ozzfest, which Sharon Osbourne started in 1996. We made a huge profit in the first year, partly because so many of the acts were willing to do it for virtually no money. The Country Music Association came over to see what I was doing and designed their own 'Fan Fair' in Nashville along exactly the same lines, which was very flattering for me. They even gave me an award as a result.

For the second year of the festival I managed to persuade BBC Television and Radio to come along and record it, which really opened us up to the world. Now we had the potential to put the acts in front of audiences of millions, not just thousands. The BBC also took over the job of building the sets, which cut down my overheads considerably. Each year things

116

got bigger and when the festival grew to four days the BBC started dividing it up into eight thirty-minute television programmes, plus a special at Christmas, and Radio Two would broadcast hour-long segments, giving the acts the most enormous amount of exposure, making their managers even keener to get them on the show. We were well and truly launched.

As the festival grew in popularity I increased its length. Starting as a one-day event it was soon two days, then three days in 1976 over a bank holiday weekend, and eventually four days. I was offering the public special deals with a twenty per cent discount on two-day tickets, which was a completely new concept at the time but is now used in most areas of theatre and showbusiness. The fans responded brilliantly.

On a night when Willie Nelson was the headline act at the festival, Nelson Mandela was due to appear at a concert held in his honour next door at Wembley Stadium. While waiting for Willie Nelson to come on stage the audience started to sing 'Willie Nelson Mandela' and the sound flooded out across the car park into the Stadium where tens of thousands of people joined in. The Wembley staff had never heard anything like it.

In 1973 Jeannie C Riley came over. She had had an immense hit with 'Harper Valley PTA' in 1968, which was the first record to get to number one simultaneously in Billboard's country and pop charts in the US and had a similar success in Europe.

Tex Ritter was a great star of country music and acting, having sung the title song for the movie *High Noon* – 'Do Not Forsake Me' – and starred in over forty 'singing cowboy' movies himself. I had arranged a big European tour for him in my early days and he used to come over to the festivals. He and his wife Dorothy, an American actress who had trained at RADA in London, became close personal friends and even after Tex died I still used to invite Dorothy over each year as a friend. She was very well connected in the Republican Party after Tex surprised everyone in 1970 by entering Tennessee's primary election for the US Senate. She was always very generous in getting me showered with praise and citations from

Congress and the Senate and she arranged for me to be awarded Freeman of the city of Nashville. In 1982 I was given the annual Tex Ritter award for services to country music. I felt confident I was making Lily proud of her boy.

★ Marriage ★

Lily, being the typical Jewish mother, was always trying to get me safely married off to a suitable woman. Since I was her only child I was also her only hope of being a grandmother, which probably fuelled her efforts even further.

One of my liaisons during the sixties had resulted in the conception of a child, but my relationship with his mother hadn't worked out and so I didn't often see my son, Damien, which must have been a source of sadness to Lily, as it was for me. In fact my mother was pretty cross with me at the time the pregnancy happened, never being someone to hold back on saying what she was thinking, which was, of course, one of the reasons I loved her as much as I did. She and Dad made a big effort to stay in touch with Damien and his mother for as long as they could.

Damien's mother was a lovely girl from Cheltenham called Sonia, who was just nineteen when I met her in the mid sixties. She was a pretty little thing but our relationship never moved on and she married someone else. I had seen Damien quite a bit when he was a baby, and went on supporting him until he was grown up, and my parents used see him until his mother died and he went off to live with his stepfather. We made contact again about ten years ago, which felt like a tying up of loose ends, but then we lost touch completely. However, I'm very happy to say that he has recently make contact with me via the facebook website and has a son, Luke, my grandson, who I'm so looking forward to meeting.

So, by the time I was thirty-four years old Lily was becoming even more determined to get the next generation of her family sorted out. I, however, was so embroiled in my working life I really didn't have the time or energy needed for courting someone properly. I was also meeting plenty of beautiful, available women because of the business I was in, none of whom required a promise of marriage before they would allow me to have my way, so I was in no hurry to settle down – all in all I had turned into every Jewish mother's nightmare from that respect. Lily was undoubtedly thrilled with the way my career and finances were going and she intended to lend the same degree of guidance to the progress of my private life.

I went round to my parents' flat for dinner one night in 1969, as I often did, after they'd just come back from a holiday in Malta.

'How was the holiday?' I enquired innocently as I shed my coat and sat down.

'We met some wonderful people,' Mum gushed. 'They've got a wonderful daughter, Laura. You must meet her.'

'Oh, don't start,' I said, just wanting a quiet evening and something to eat after a hard day's work.

'No, no,' she insisted. 'She's a beautiful girl.'

'Have you seen her?'

'No, I haven't seen her.'

'Then how do you know she's a beautiful girl?'

'They've told me,' she replied, in a voice that suggested I was stupid to even ask. 'She's a singer, that's how we got talking. I told them all about you. I'm going to phone them up now, tell them you're here.'

'Don't do that, Mum,' I pleaded, but it was too late – she was already dialling.

'Hello, Eileen? It's Lily. I've got my son here this evening ... Really?'

I soon gathered that this unseen daughter was, co-incidentally, with her mother as well that evening.

'Let them speak,' Mum was saying.

'Mum!' I protested – and later discovered Laura was reacting in exactly the same way at the other end of the line.

Neither of the mothers, however, was willing to let us get away with it. We were both forced to take over the phones. Because Laura was a professional singer she had already heard

120

my name. I asked her about her singing, not knowing what else to say in the circumstances.

'As a matter of fact, I'm on television tonight,' she told me. 'On the *Roy Castle Show*.'

'I'll give it a watch then,' I said, 'and call you afterwards.'

After dinner I sat with my parents watching Roy Castle, who was a big name in family entertainment at the time as a dancer, singer and musician. His show basically followed the old-fashioned Saturday night variety format and Laura came on as one half of a duet with another girl.

I had to admit, even though I was loathe to encourage my mother in her machinations, Laura was a stunning-looking girl. Her singing wasn't bad either. I rang her back after the show to compliment her on her performance and suggested in passing that she come to a recording session I had booked for one of my groups the next day.

'Maybe we could put something on tape,' I suggested casually. I'm sure both mothers were purring happily by that stage.

Laura duly turned up at the studio the next day but the session with the group overran and I wasn't able to fit her in.

'I'm so sorry,' I said when it became obvious we had run out of time. 'Can I take you out to dinner to make amends for wasting your time?'

'Oh, that would be very nice,' she said.

I then had to admit that my Aston Martin had gone into the garage for a service and I would need a lift home. I couldn't imagine that I was doing too well at making a good first impression, but she brushed aside my apologies. I still lived in Canonbury and she lived in Wimbledon, which is completely in the opposite direction, so she took me to my flat, went back home on the other side of London and then came to get me again, without any complaints. I was beginning to think that maybe my mother wasn't such a bad judge of women, even ones she hadn't met.

That evening Laura and I got on brilliantly and embarked on a whirlwind romance which resulted in us getting married at Caxton Hall about three months after our first meeting, with our reception held in the Carlton Towers Hotel in Sloane

121

Street. Laura was a kind, understanding woman as well as being beautiful. I was infatuated and I also thought (encouraged by Lily's enthusiasm, no doubt) that she would make a good mother for my future children. She came from a lovely family. My father-in-law was a nice man whose family ran a company called Symonds Engineering, manufacturers of copper wiring. He had a great many siblings and all the brothers worked together in the same business. He and I even started a little company together selling mail-order merchandise from a showroom in Victoria. One of my brothers-in-law, a dancer called Rodney, worked for us there. The merchandise we were selling was all stuff that I had got the rights to in America, like a 'how to play the guitar' book by Chet Atkins and cowboy hats. It was stuff that I would sell at the festivals, which needed another outlet during the rest of the year. We actually had a lot of trouble with the Chet Atkins product because the packagers had included a guitar pick loose in the box, which scratched the records in transit and meant we had to refund hundreds of customers. I think I've still got a stack of the things in a warehouse somewhere.

Chet was considered by many to be the greatest electric guitar player in the world so he didn't want to appear in the festival, believing he could fill Wembley on his own, backed by a symphony orchestra. It was going to be the first time a major orchestra had played country and I wasn't too sure we would be able to fill such a big venue. Since I was organizing a European tour for him anyway I added Wembley to the itinerary because I liked the concept of teaming him with an orchestra and because the record company agreed to underwrite it. Chet was a very powerful man at RCA Records, even owning the building that they occupied in Nashville, and had been instrumental in bringing them into country. I was proved right, however, about Wembley, and we only managed to sell around half the nine thousand seats. The rest of the tour, however, which was played out in smaller venues, was a big success and Chet was a nice man to work with.

Laura's father introduced me into his livery company, which led to me being made a Freeman of the City of London, and to the splendid Royal Automobile Club in Pall Mall. He taught me a lot, knocking off some of the rougher edges that I still retained from my upbringing and from my early days in business despite the work that Joe had already done on polishing me up.

Lily had achieved her objective of marrying me off well and Laura was very understanding about the demands my business made on my time. Although by then I was well established in my career and had managed to get some money in the bank, right from the start our marriage had to fit in with my hectic and unpredictable work schedule. The morning after the wedding I had to go into the office and Laura went back to her mother's house to wait until we could set out to America on our honeymoon three days later. The trip was going to be a mixture of holiday and business as we were going to be attending the Country Music Awards Ceremony in Nashville and I was going to be rushing around making arrangements for the 1970 Wembley festival.

The Country Music Awards Ceremony is now a giant global television show to rival the Oscars, and it was a big deal even then. Laura was ambitious for a career as a singer herself, so she was more forgiving of having her honeymoon mixed in with business than many new brides would have been. In Nashville she enjoyed the adventure as much as I did, being feted everywhere we went because of the success of my first festival at Wembley the year before, and we were also invited to dinner at Johnny and June's house, which was a pretty cool way for any man to be able to impress his new bride. Everyone in Nashville could now see that if the Wembley festival became a regular annual event we could all make a lot of money from spin-off tours, record sales and publishing rights – even the people who had been sceptical when I first arrived in their town. Laura was quite shocked by how backward things still were in that part of America. It was the third time I'd been there so I was getting fairly used to it, but my blushing young bride was shocked to be casually asked 'How do you deal with your niggers back in England?' by the local Chief of Police.

Before going to Nashville we flew first into New York and had what we thought was a dinner date almost as soon as we arrived with Freddy Bienstock, a big music producer, at his Park Avenue apartment. Freddy was particularly important at that time because he handled all of Elvis's music publishing. The year before Elvis had staged his big 'comeback' television special, which had re-established his credibility in the eyes of the world as a singer after the string of lucrative but laughable movies that his famous manager, Colonel Tom Parker, had locked him into during the sixties. The whole world, which had been distracted by Beatlemania and everything that followed, had suddenly been reminded of just what a great singer and star the man was.

Still jet lagged from the flight, Laura and I got ourselves ready at the glamorous Pierre Hotel beside Central Park and headed off to Freddy's magnificent apartment, where we were plied with endless Martinis but no food at all, which meant we were reeling merrily back up the road to the Pierre a few hours later.

The introduction paid off, however, because around 1972 Freddy arranged an introduction for me with Colonel Parker, so that I could try to persuade him to allow me to take Elvis to Europe for a tour. I knew that if I could get his agreement I could fill any number of venues and I offered to pay him a hundred thousand dollars a show, certain that I would be able to recoup virtually any outlay. The Colonel was very pleasant and we met in hotel suite in Las Vegas. He told me he would think about my offer but eventually he turned it down. I was later told that the reason he never brought Elvis to Europe was because he (the Colonel that is) had collaborated with the Germans during the war and was frightened he would be arrested. I have also heard that he was worried America would not let him back in if he ever went abroad, because he was Dutch and had never got the correct paperwork for living and working in the States. Now that both the Colonel and Elvis are dead I doubt we will ever be able to extricate the truth from all the myths, many of which I'm sure the Colonel built up himself to increase the mystique surrounding his great star.

Music managers come in all shapes and sizes, and another larger-than-life character was Michael Levy. I first met him when he had a record label called Magnet and his main star was a performer called Alvin Stardust. Alvin, who was born Bernard Jewry, had also sung under the name of Shane Fenton after the first Shane Fenton died from an illness left over from his childhood just before his group was offered an audition by the BBC. The group then asked Bernard, who was working for them as a roadie, to take over and the original Shane's mother asked him to take the same stage name in memory of her son. They had a series of hits before the group disbanded and Bernard re-invented himself yet again as Alvin, becoming one of the big acts of the glam rock era.

Many years later Michael would go on to become Lord Levy, chief fundraiser for the Labour Party, close friend and tennis partner of Tony Blair and a major player in a 'cash for honours' scandal. He was famous for being a tough business-man right from the start. Pete Waterman has been quoted as saying he was the greatest salesman he had ever met: 'He could sell sand to the Arabs.'

Before Alvin had his first hit negotiations to get him to do a tour with me went on for a couple of weeks.

'What happens', I asked Michael, 'if we don't have a hit by the time the tour starts?'

'Don't worry,' Michael assured me, 'we will.'

There was a lot of talk and rumour about chart fixing around that time and I never quite worked out what Michael did, but Alvin had his first hit, 'My Coo Ca Choo', just in time, as promised, and a new star was born.

Being a music promoter must be a good training ground for politicians because another big promoter in Ireland in the seventies was Albert Reynolds, who went on to become the country's Prime Minister and a prime mover in the Northern Ireland peace process. His family owned about fourteen dance halls and one of his biggest successes was in bringing Jim

Reeves over for a tour in 1963 at the same time that President Kennedy was visiting.

One of the most important music promoters in Ireland was Jim Aitken, a great friend and a gentleman. He used to book out some of the Wembley acts in Ireland for me, including Johnny Cash. Not once in over thirty years did we have a cross word or were the takings even a penny short. He was always renowned for his generosity and honesty. Sadly, Jim died in 2007, and I lost a true and dear friend.

Once we were back in London after our honeymoon Laura and I moved into my flat in Canonbury, making it our first marital home. It wasn't long, however, before it became obvious that she wasn't going to be happy living there. I could understand that. It was a nice bachelor flat in a modern Georgian-style block, but not right for a married couple thinking of starting a family.

'I'd like to buy a house in Wimbledon,' she told me when I asked what she wanted to do.

I was happy to move wherever she chose in London because things were going well for me and I knew that she wanted to be closer to her family. I was a north London boy and knew nothing about that side of the city, but Laura went house hunting and found a lovely property with a big garden in Burghley Road, backing on to the All England Tennis courts. I took my mother over to see it since I always consulted her on virtually every decision I made, and she was just as keen on the house as Laura was. It was on the market for £28,800, which was a great deal of money in 1970, especially as it needed a lot doing to it, and I was going to need to borrow some money to buy it. Because I had been building the business I hadn't been drawing a high salary, putting all the profits from each venture back into funding the next one, which meant it was hard to persuade anyone to give me a mortgage. I could see Laura had set her heart on the property so I got my accountant to buff up my figures a bit and I managed to borrow twice what I needed so that we could set about renovating it as soon as we owned it. The deal was done and we moved in with the builders.

Forty years later, after almost doubling the size of the house, I was offered five and a half million pounds for it by developers, a good return on the original investment, especially as it served as a wonderful family home throughout that time. Laura and I had four children there: Oliver, who arrived within a year of us moving to Wimbledon, quickly followed by Scarlett, Joseph and Charity.

Over the years our family became very involved in the Wimbledon community. I did a lot of fund raising for the local synagogue and was eventually put in charge of buying a new one on nearby Parkside. Wimbledon became my village, just as it was Laura's.

While we were settling into Wimbledon, Mum and Dad stayed on in their old flat in North London, but I would still go up to see them at every opportunity, and I still confided everything that was going on in my life to Lily, listening to her advice in the same way I always had. As Oliver got older I used to take him up there on Saturdays because I had three season tickets to the Arsenal and I would either take him and Dad, or Uncle Mick and him, or I would leave Oliver with Mum and go to the football with the other two.

In the mid seventies, once I was able to afford it, I bought Mum and Dad a flat in Kingston, overlooking the river, and moved them down to be closer to us. Mick had died by then and Dad went back to driving a black cab until he had a miniature stroke and his health started to deteriorate seriously.

I felt very proud of everything I was achieving, both in my business and with my family. Life was hard work, but the rewards were good.

★ Majorcan ★ ★ Variety

As the business grew and new opportunities presented themselves, I didn't limit myself to the worlds of rock and roll and country music. I was happy to put on any shows that I thought the public would like. One of the things that Joe Collins had done when he was younger was organize touring versions of famous radio shows. I continued the idea when there was a successful television drama series about the Strauss family, starring actors like Derek Jacobi and Jane Seymour, which had caught the public's imagination. The series was owned by Lew Grade so I bought the rights off him and then hired the London Symphony Orchestra for a concert tour. *Till Death Us Do Part* was a big hit television series in the late sixties and early seventies. It starred a friend of mine, Warren Mitchell as Alf Garnett and we put on a live show called *The Thoughts of Chairman Alf*. Warren and I used to go to football together, even though he supported a different team. I did another tour with the Royal Scots Guards and another with violinist, Stephane Grappelli.

At the end of the seventies a programme called *New Faces* was the *Britain's Got Talent* of its time. Like *BGT*, it was a television talent show in which judges pronounced on the acts, sometimes being very cutting. I organized a live tour for the stars that emerged from it, people like Les Dennis and many other names who have long since sunk back into obscurity, just as Simon Cowell does with his protégés today.

I was still doing traditional variety shows as well, like when I secured the rights from the ABC Blackpool and the ABC Yarmouth to put on Sunday concerts, and I hired acts as varied as Wizard and Rolf Harris, Ted Rogers and Leo Sayer, Dorothy Squires and Max Bygraves, Ken Dodd and Reg Varney, Mike Yarwood and Peters and Lee. The list went on forever. The worst thing about working with Ken Dodd (who was a massive star by that stage, having come from the music hall traditions of stand-up and having got himself into the *Guinness Book of Records* for the longest ever joke telling session: 1,500 jokes in three and a half hours) was that he would always overrun his allotted time. Once he got started he never wanted to stop and the audience was happy to encourage him to keep rambling on because he was so funny. The problem for me was that whenever he did that I would be landed with big theatre bills as a result. Ken also had a good singing voice and sold over a million copies of his biggest hit, a ballad written in the thirties called 'Tears', and did almost as well with another catchy number titled 'Happiness'.

For four months I put on all the shows that went into the Wimbledon Theatre, booking names like Leslie Crowther, Syd Lawrence and his orchestra, Freda Payne, Spike Milligan and the Royal Philharmonic Orchestra. These were true variety shows in the traditional mould. In the summer I took the Prince's Theatre in Torquay and put on stars like Larry Grayson, Ted Rogers, Des O'Connor and Bruce Forsyth. I also followed Joe's tradition of putting on pantomimes in places as far apart as Ipswich and Southampton, Peterborough and Portsmouth. Pantomime was never my great love, as it was for Joe, but if I thought I could sell tickets for an event then I was willing to give it a go. My old friend Barbara Windsor used to star for me, and Christopher Biggins, another friend later crowned 'King of the Jungle' on *I'm a Celebrity* ...

It is easy to forget sometimes how much things have changed over the last twenty or thirty years. One of the artists I brought over from America was Rod McKuen, the poet, composer and singer. Virtually every woman in the country seemed to have a bit of crush on him at the time, including my wife, which was why it was a shock to walk into his dressing room and find him holding hands with his boyfriend, the movie star Rock Hudson, who at that time was also still firmly in the closet and stayed there until shortly before he died of Aids in 1985.

A huge amount of my energy had to go into the country festival simply because the scale of the show became so enormous. Once I had proved how successful the format could be I was able to go after sponsors for the event and managed to convince Marlborough cigarettes to come on board. The problem then was that they overstepped the mark with the BBC, who were very strict about anything to do with advertising and product promotion. Marlborough upset them by slapping their distinctive red and white logo all over the steps of the stage about an hour before the broadcast was due to go out. If they had been allowed to get away with it, it would have been great free advertising for them, worth millions, but when the BBC officials spotted it they threatened to cancel the broadcast unless we got rid of it. There was then a desperate rush to paint over the logos in time for the cameras to go live. That wasn't the end of the matter either. Once the event was all over and the BBC had had time to consider the situation, they informed me that they would pull out if Marlborough came back as a sponsor the following year. The BBC was in a strong bargaining position as I couldn't afford to lose their coverage and so I reluctantly had to turn Marlborough's repeat business away. Luckily I managed to persuade Silk Cut to fill the void and they were much better at handling the BBC because they were part of Benson and Hedges and already sponsored the golf and the cricket and the show jumping at Hickstead. They understood how carefully the sponsorship game needed to be played. They stayed with me for five years after that, to enormous mutual benefit.

When Merle Haggard was appearing he wanted to open his set with one of his biggest hits, 'Okie from Muskogee', which starts with the line 'We don't smoke marijuana in Muskogee,' which the BBC wanted him to change. Willie Nelson's band played Merle's introduction and he was introduced, but nothing happened. The band kept playing, but still no sign of Merle. The stage manager ran to his dressing room to find him on the phone to Heathrow trying to get on the next available flight home. I was called in to try to calm things down but Merle was adamant – he wanted to sing 'his' song and there was no room for negotiation. I quickly went back to the BBC and arranged for them to let him sing on the understanding that they would cut it from their broadcast later.

Once the BBC was involved we really had to run to tight schedules, finishing the shows exactly when we were contracted to. It was always a problem with the artists because, like Ken Dodd, if they were getting a good reaction from the audience they never wanted to come off stage. There was one time when I actually had to go out on to the stage myself, put my arm around the artist's shoulder and steer him off. I'd often had to do the same with Jerry Lee Lewis when he was on tour for me playing smaller venues, and was just as likely to run over time as he was to run under time and leave the audience feeling angry and short-changed.

'Jerry,' I would say if we had run out of time and he looked like he was about to start into another song, 'it's time for us to have a drink.'

It never worried me, walking out on to a stage, even in front of giant crowds. I guess I was still a frustrated performer at heart and probably always will be.

I was constantly on the lookout for new business opportunities and in 1970 I went to a music conference in Palma, Majorca, a destination that was becoming increasingly popular with British holiday makers. During a break in business I went for a walk along the promenade to get some fresh air and came across a new-looking building that appeared to be a theatre. The doors were open to the sunshine so I wandered inside and came into a beautiful, deserted 2,000-seat auditorium. As I stood there, gazing around me, a man of about my age appeared beside me, speaking in Spanish.

'I'm sorry,' I said, 'I don't speak Spanish.'

'Do you like the theatre?' he said, switching easily to English.

'I think it's wonderful.'

'It belongs to my father.'

'What do you do here?'

'We do classical concerts and operettas all through the winter.'

'What do you do with it in the summer?'

'We close it.'

I couldn't believe what I was hearing. Tourists were pouring into Majorca with money to burn and a need to be entertained and he was closing his doors?

'Do you think you would be interested in renting it to me in the summer?' I asked.

'I will ask my father,' he said, taking my name and the hotel where I was staying.

Later that day the phone rang in my room and my new friend asked if I would like to meet his father, who turned out to be just as charming as his son. I explained to both of them I would like to rent the theatre between June and September.

'That would be good,' the old man said, 'because our season runs from the end of September to April.'

Once he had met me, the father was happy to let me deal with his son from then on. I signed up for one year, with an option for a further five years and first refusal for a further five years after that. I then started negotiating with a number of companies who I knew were good at running theatres, including Bernard Delfont, who I had met and got to know through Joe. Bernard was Lew and Leslie Grade's brother and was just as successful. As well as putting on hundreds of shows, including *Stop the World – I Want to Get Off* and *Sweet Charity*, he also converted the Hippodrome into the famous Talk of the Town restaurant with Harold Davison, where acts like Judy Garland, Frank Sinatra, Shirley Bassey and Eartha Kitt famously performed. He was also chief executive of EMI and ended up as Lord Delfont, frequently seen ushering Her Majesty the Queen and other royals into the Royal Variety Show. The advantage of doing business with Bernie, I thought, was that he controlled a lot of the British talent and would be able to help with the bookings. It was in my mind that I would try to set up a partnership deal with him once I had got everything organized in Palma and had something more concrete to offer him.

I was starting to book some of the talent already, to ensure that I had a show lined up and ready, regardless of who I ended up in partnership with. I booked a lot of big names of the time: Clodagh Rodgers, (who was then performing 'Jack in the Box' in the Eurovision Song Contest and ended up running a wine bar in Wimbledon), Susan Maughan, (who sang the huge 1962 hit 'I Wanna be Bobby's Girl'), the comedian Lance Percival, Matt Munro, Herman's Hermits, Georgie Fame, Alan Price, Nina and Frederick, Marmalade, Vince Hill and Harry Secombe. The idea was to have one big star each week aimed at the British market, with supporting acts, going back again to the idea of a traditional variety show. I wanted to make these the sort of shows that the whole family would want to go to while they were on holiday and old-fashioned variety was a tried-and-tested formula that I was comfortable with.

As I finalized my arrangements for Bernie Delfont to be my partner I was learning fast by doing everything myself, getting posters printed and booking sites to display them, selling tickets and all the other aspects of putting on a show, which I usually left to other people with more experience. I had employed people out in Palma to organize the publicity as well as the technical aspects like lighting and sound. The wage bill was starting to grow but I didn't worry too much because I was sure we were going to be able to fill the place virtually every night. It was an enjoyable project to be working on, but it was also hard work, particularly because this was all happening alongside the preparations for the next country festival and all the other tours that I was organizing at the same time. On top of everything else, Laura was going to be giving birth to Oliver, our first child, at pretty much the same moment the Spanish theatre was due to open, which obviously I hadn't planned for, so that was adding to the pressure.

I was flying back and forth to Spain a lot during the preparations, but I was going to have to ensure that I was home in London for Oliver's birth on the actual opening day, leaving all the arrangements in Majorca in the hands of Cyril Smith. All the early shows were sold out now, so I was feeling confident that it was going to go well and that Cyril would be able to handle everything on my behalf.

Laura was booked into a Catholic hospital called St Theresa's and Oliver made his entrance on time. Once the birth was over I went home, feeling high on the idea of being a new father and having a baby whose life I was going to be able to become involved with, when I received a call from someone on my staff in Palma.

'You'd better get back here right away,' they told me, 'you won't believe what's happened.'

'What's happened?'

'The police have closed the theatre down and arrested Cyril. The local clubs and restaurants have put a denuncio on you.'

'What the hell is a denuncio?'

These were the last days of General Franco's rule, when Spain had very different laws from Britain. One of them, I was now told, was that if a foreigner was thought to be taking customers away from local business people, they could put a 'denuncio' on you and close you down. It was the first I had heard of such a law. The local clubs in Palma, however, had noticed that their bookings were all falling away from the first week that the theatre was opening and realized it was because the tourists were booking to go to my shows instead of theirs. A complaint had been lodged and the police had walked into the theatre in the middle of rehearsals and closed everything down. There were now chains on the doors and no one was allowed in.

I flew straight back to Palma, leaving Laura and Oliver in the hospital, and bailed Cyril out of jail. I did a lot of shouting at the lawyers who were supposed to be advising me, wanting to know why nobody had told me about this law, and received a lot of disinterested shrugs. They had definitely been negligent, but what was I going to do? Was I going to sue a lawyer in Spain while Franco was in power? It didn't seem likely that was going to achieve anything beyond creating more expenses for myself. It looked like I was just going to have to bite the bullet and cancel the whole operation. I immediately came back to London and found the story was all over the newspapers and there was a phone message waiting for me from Bernie Delfont, suggesting that I should go round to tell him what was happening.

I walked over to his offices, which were above the Prince of Wales Theatre at the time, feeling a bit sorry for myself. It looked like my whole empire was going to crumble around me just because of this one basic mistake. By going into a market I didn't know I had overreached myself in a way I hadn't done since I set up the ill-advised restaurant in Hanover Square. The day before everything had looked rosy with a sell-out season on the way and a healthy new baby son. Now, just a few hours later, nothing was certain any more.

Apart from this one liability my business was solid but I was in desperate need of cash to pay off all the acts I had booked, and everyone else who had been working so hard for me. Off the top of my head I reckoned I needed about £20,000 just to stay in business till the next week, which at that time was almost the price of a detached house in Wimbledon.

Bernie welcomed me into his office and listened impassively as I told him the whole sorry tale.

'Well,' he said when I finished. 'What is it that you need, Mervyn?'

'I need twenty thousand pounds, Bernie' I said.

He nodded his understanding, opened the top drawer of his desk, took out a cheque book and started writing.

'There's the £20,000,' he said, tearing it out and passing it across. 'If you get the theatre open we're partners; if you don't, then you pay me back over five years, interest at the bank rate. Now go and sort yourself out.'

Of course, I never managed to get the theatre open, but Bernie had saved my skin that day and I was able to pay him back as arranged over the next five years as the rest of my business continued to grow, bringing in the cash flow I needed to pay for my mistake. The owner of the theatre in Palma also took pity on me and let me off the rent, which I was very grateful for.

136

Cyril Smith, who had been left holding the can while I was in England welcoming Oliver into the world, was a great friend. He used to live with an actress called Yootha Joyce, who was very successful on television in a comedy series in the late seventies called *Man About the House*, in which she played the landlady who lived downstairs from a bunch of young people sharing a flat. She and her on-screen husband, played by Brian Murphy, were then given their own show called *George and Mildred*, which was another huge hit, making her a household name and face. Laura and I became very friendly with Cyril and Yootha and it was a terrible tragedy when she died in 1980, while still only in her early fifties.

I used to rely on Cyril to do all sorts of things for me and when Slim Whitman asked if I would arrange for him to do a tour of Australia and New Zealand I asked Cyril to go over and set it up for me. I gave him fifty thousand dollars for all the set-up expenses. On the way down to Australia, however, he stopped over in Bangkok, met a girl and disappeared off to Australia with her and with my money. I never saw him again but I heard he got himself a job with Kerry Packer, who was one of the world's most colourful media moguls and had just set up World Series Cricket. I was told that Cyril was running all the entertainment side of the business for him. By that time I had been to court often enough to know that there was little chance I would ever be able to get my money back without spending a lot more than fifty thousand dollars on lawyers, so yet again I had to let it go, but I was shocked that someone who had always been so loyal should change so radically. Every day I was learning new lessons about the business world and about the people in it.

⋆ Furthering
⋆ The Festival ⋆

Once the country festival had been established for a couple of years fans started to ask if they could book their tickets a year in advance, so I set up a booth at the show, taking anything up to twenty thousand pounds in deposits before we even knew who was going to appear the following year. We had managed to build such a good reputation for persuading the best people in the world to perform that the punters were willing to take us on trust.

It was always a wonderful feeling to be inside the arena at Wembley at a high point of the festival and to be able to look around at ten thousand people enjoying something that I had thought up and made happen, something that was going out through the cameras and microphones to millions more. It made me feel like I had really achieved something worthwhile. It was an incredible high.

One of the greatest thrills came from discovering a new talent for the first time and then seeing their career take off. I didn't just book the established names: sometimes I would hear of new, up-and-coming stars, which was what happened with Emmylou Harris, and they would be able to break into the European market through appearing at the festival. Emmylou first came over in 1976 to tour for me, including two nights at the Odeon Hammersmith, which was another first for country music, and we struck up a good friendship. I even flew all the way out to her home in San Francisco one time to talk about her touring plans, not something I would have done for many performers.

I was at a party in Nashville one time and there was a record of a man singing in the background. Liking what I heard, I asked who he was and someone told me his name was Don Williams. The next day I did some investigation, found out who his agent was and put in a call. Within an hour or two of me making contact with him the agent was round in my office eager to hear what I might be offering.

'I like your guy,' I told him. 'I'm going to make him a big star in Britain.'

Before I brought Don over to Europe I went to see ABC, who were his record company in Britain, to talk to a guy called Ian Rafini. Ian wasn't that interested in country music, like a lot of the music establishment of the time, seeing it as old fashioned and corny and not as glamorous as pop and rock and roll.

'You've got this guy on your books called Don Williams,' I told him.

'This isn't one of your country acts is it, Mervyn?' he sighed.

'Just listen,' I said, and played Don singing 'You're My Best Friend'.

'I'm bringing him over to perform at the festival,' I went on, 'and if you release this record at the same time I guarantee you will have a top ten hit.'

Ian reluctantly agreed and it happened exactly as I predicted. Appearing at the festival gave him a platform to promote the record and it went into the charts, making a major star out of Don and a classic from the song.

Don was one of the performers, like George Hamilton IV and Johnny Cash, who became a good friend through us working together. We played golf and our families got together a lot whenever I arranged solo tours for him after his festival debut. Don had initially been with a big agent called Jim Halsey, who was based in Tulsa and used to stage his own events in the city as well as looking after talent like Don and Tammy Wynette. The Nashville establishment resented Jim, mainly because he came from Tulsa, which they saw as a rival city, but I liked him and signed a million dollar deal with him in the eighties to bring all his artists over for tours and festivals at a time when many of the agents over there still hadn't seen the potential of the European market for their artists, and he became a good friend. News that I had spent that much money with an agent from Tulsa put a lot of people's backs up in Nashville. Jim's father-in-law was a famous America Indian artist and Jim gave me several of his original paintings which hang proudly on my office walls to this day. Jim eventually gave up the business and became a university lecturer in California, in the subject of entertainment.

It has often been my experience, however, that once a star begins to build up an entourage around them you start having trouble because of clashes of egos and people wanting to prove their usefulness to their employer in order to justify their salary. One of the venues I had Don booked into was a civic place called Bingley Hall. It held about three thousand people but had chairs that weren't fixed to the floor and moved about, making it hard to control and impossible to be sure how many people were in the room. Don had an entourage with him by then and when we gave them the returns for the night his management accused me of short-changing them on the seating.

'You think I'm trying to steal a few seats from you?' I asked. 'Are you crazy? The chairs move around, we only know the number of tickets we sold. Do you think I would jeopardize my relationship with Don after all these years for the sake of fifty chairs?'

They had made up their minds that I was trying to cheat them and there was nothing I could do to convince them otherwise. The more I protested the worse it sounded and they managed to convince Don that I was lying, so he never toured with me again, which made me very sad. Sometimes, in business as in other areas of life, there is just nothing you can do to stop a relationship breaking down.

One man who always acknowledged that it was the Wembley festival that made him a star and stayed grateful to the end was Boxcar Willie. His name was originally Lecil Travis Martin and he took the name Boxcar Willie from a character in one of

141

his songs. He was in the US Air Force to start with and told me that he had always dreamed of appearing at Wembley. I liked his music and booked him and he was an overnight sensation. He had become a star overnight and I was able to set up tours for him, during which we became good friends. I once invited him and Johnny Russell, another star who was touring with him, for dinner at Joe Allen's, the fashionable burger joint in London's Covent Garden. Boxcar insisted on paying, even though I had been the one doing the inviting. That very seldom happened and I was touched by the gesture. He was a lovely man to work with. Johnny Russell was the same, always insisting on taking me out to dinner whenever I was in Nashville. As both a singer and a comedian Johnny was immensely popular with the festival crowds, who were hard to please when it came to comedy. His songs were covered by everyone from Jim Reeves to Buck Owens, and one of his songs, 'Act Naturally', was even covered by The Beatles on their *Help* album. It is said to have sold more than thirty million copies in various versions.

Once the festival was established every singer seemed to want to get into it and I was constantly being approached by performers and their representatives. An Irish singer called Rose-Marie had been asking for a while and when someone else recommended that I should listen to her I invited her to the office in London. She lived in Blackpool and I was touring with Don at the time, so we agreed to meet again for dinner in Manchester so she could give me a tape. We got on well and I agreed to put her into the next festival, where she was a huge success with the audience. I got her a couple of television appearances on shows like *Celebrity Squares* and we made an album with her. She was moving up the ladder and I agreed to become her full-time manager, which was a role I never really enjoyed with any of the artists.

Anyway, I got Rose-Marie booked into the Sporting Club in Monte Carlo for a three-week cabaret season. I would fly down to Nice and then take the helicopter into Monte Carlo to watch the show. On one of these visits the manager took me to one side to tell me that Rose-Marie had started to tell jokes in her act rather than sing. Since she had a strong Irish accent most of the international Monaco audience had no idea what she was talking about.

'Can you ask her please to just stick to the songs?' he asked.

Over dinner that night I told her that she needed to cut down the comedy, but I had created a monster and she thought she knew what was best for her act and that was the way she wanted to develop it. I thought things were getting out of hand and so when she got back to London I told her I couldn't handle her any more because she was refusing to listen to the advice I was giving.

The festival had grown into a huge money spinner and I wanted to extend the franchise and spread my net wider. The board of the Country Music Association had come to London for one of their meetings at the time the festival was on and were so impressed they went back to Nashville and copied my format exactly, calling it Fan Festival, and invited me to join them as International Vice President. Their festival is still going today and has grown into a huge multi-million dollar business. I didn't mind them copying me because I had already tried to set up something similar over there in America myself and found it hard because I was competing with all the local state fairs. For me to take the format there myself was like carting coals to Newcastle, so it was much better that they did it themselves.

I knew, however, the record companies and artists' managers were keen to get their acts seen in other European countries apart from Britain and since I had gone to the trouble to get them all into the same place at the same time it seemed sensible to look for other outlets for the festival, which would reach new audiences and sell more tickets. I looked around Europe for other places where I could move the whole show on to, chartering a plane to carry everyone from one venue to another.

We had now become like an army on the move. I started with Gothenburg in Sweden because I had a friend there who was an agent and was able to represent me, selling exhibition space around the perimeter and getting a sponsor just like in

London. The reaction from the public was good, I think partly because in Gothenburg they could pick up programmes put out by the BBC and so people were already aware of the British version of the festival and already had a taste for some of the artists. We sold eleven thousand tickets, making £52,000 from that alone.

By the eighth festival I was starting to broaden the base to include more contemporary performers like the Ozark Mountain Daredevils and Buffy Sainte-Marie, which upset some of the country purists who didn't want too much folk or rock and roll cross-over, but I needed to keep moving forward and looking for acts that would attract new audiences.

I looked outside Europe as well and at one stage I met with David Frost, who was doing a lot of work in Australia at the time, because I thought he would be a good person to take the festival down there with me. He was a huge media figure at the time, a bit like Simon Cowell is now, constantly jetting around the world from one show to another. We met in Las Vegas and both became quite enthusiastic about the plan. I even spent a couple of weeks in Australia myself doing newspaper and radio interviews before I realized that I was biting off more than I could chew. Australia was simply too far away for me to be able to control everything in the way I needed to and David was even busier than I was. I didn't have anyone down there I could hand the whole thing over to so I called it off.

I thought about organizing a festival in South Africa too, after being approached by some guys called the Petra Brothers, who were big promoters from Johannesburg, and I went there with George Hamilton IV to see what the options were. South Africa seemed a much better bet geographically than Australia as long as we could set up several different venues to make it worthwhile for the stars to fly all the way down there, and I started to sort these out. But these were the days of apartheid, when Nelson Mandela was still imprisoned on Robben Island and South Africa was blacklisted by most Western countries. Being so wrapped up in the business of putting on shows I had no interest in international politics and stumbled ahead without any idea of what deep water I was getting myself into. Within

144

twenty-four hours of the press release going out to announce the concerts, I got a call from a guy I knew at the Musicians' Union.

'Mervyn,' he said, 'you can't take your festival to South Africa.'

'Why not?'

'Because we'll blacklist you.'

'How are you going to blacklist me in South Africa?'

'You don't understand, Mervyn. We'll blacklist you over *here*. We'll oppose all your applications for musicians coming into Britain. And I'm going to ring Equity now as well and they'll do the same.'

Now he had me, because bringing American stars into Britain was my main source of business. If they weren't allowed to perform here was finished.

'You wouldn't do that,' I said, now feeling very nervous, 'would you?'

'Just watch me.'

The next thing I knew I received a letter from Equity confirming that if I took my show to South Africa they would be opposing any work permits for incoming artists from America. I had to bow to the political pressure and in many ways I was happy to, having had a small taste of racism during my early visits to America. I decided to concentrate my efforts on developing the European venues, where everywhere was just a few hours' flying time from London.

At the peak of the business, when the festival was the biggest country music event in the world, I was putting on six events a year around Europe. We would start with four days at Wembley, then fly the whole show to Sweden and Norway, Holland, Berlin and Frankfurt (where there were around half a million American troops stationed at the time, giving us an almost ready-made market), finishing in Switzerland for two days. We even got as far as Spain and Italy by the end.

The Swiss are avid country fans and their festivals were the biggest after Wembley. Needless to say, the Swiss organized everything to perfection. I even had a legitimate Swiss bank account to run the whole thing from and Marlborough came back as our sponsors over there since the BBC wasn't involved.

For most of the journeys I would charter planes, but to get everyone from Frankfurt to Zurich I would hire a few carriages of a train instead, taking them on a spectacular trip through the Alps. I did it partly for my own pleasure because I loved travelling around Europe. It reminded me of when I was a twelve year old in Brussels and first got a taste for life outside England, and of the time when I was hustling encyclopedias in Cannes. It was like I had come full circle. If I had known during those lean times in Cannes how well everything would turn out I could have spared myself a lot of anxiety and just enjoyed the adventure without worrying about what the future held for me. In a way I had come back to my roots, back to the days when my maternal grandfather travelled around Europe with the circus. I now had my own country circus, which wasn't all that different a concept when it came down to it – just performing singers and musicians instead of acrobats and animals.

It was always great to be putting on a show near to American army bases because this guaranteed us a certain amount of interest before we even started our marketing efforts. The down side of that, however, was that if the troops were confined to barracks at any time we would be left with a lot of empty seats. I remember one occasion when I was standing in a mighty hall, where the Nazis had once held giant rallies, staring at rows of empty seats.

'Fuck,' I said, not realizing how close I was standing to an open mic. 'What does it take to fill this place? Adolf Hitler?'

At least it made the artists laugh, if not the Germans.

We did part of the festival in France one year, with everyone staying in the village of Sancerre. The French have very different musical tastes from most of the other European countries but they still enjoyed acts like the Everly Brothers (who'd had a lot of big worldwide hits like 'Bye Bye, Love' 'Wake Up Little Susie' and 'All I Have to Do is Dream'), although we could only take Don because he and his brother,

Phil, weren't talking by then. The French also liked Emmylou Harris, Carl Perkins and Jerry Lee Lewis, whose biggest hits, 'Great Balls of Fire' and 'A Whole Lotta Shakin' Going On', were famous all over the world.

When we got to the venue I was surprised to discover that there were television cameras everywhere. When I pointed out that they didn't have the rights to film my artists there was a lot of Gallic shrugging. I stood firm, which caused an outburst of Gallic indignation when I suggested they could have the television rights for fifty thousand dollars.

'We can't do that,' their spokesman protested, 'we have no dollars here.'

'Francs will be fine,' I said. 'It's twelve o'clock now and I'll come back at three for the money.'

By the time I came back the table in front of them was covered in money.

'So now', they said as I scooped it up, 'can we have the rights to the French-speaking countries?'

'You didn't ask me that before, did you?' I said. 'That's another discussion. I tell you what; I will let you have it for all the French-speaking territories except Canada.'

After a lot more shouting and arm waving the deal was done and the concert was able to go ahead.

In the mid eighties I did a deal with Metromedia, an American television company, as well as the BBC and they wanted a presenter who would be recognizable to the American public. We hired Patrick Duffy, who was a huge star at the time because of his role as Bobby Ewing in *Dallas*. Marie Osmond came over by herself that year, which was the first time I had hired her without her brothers, and Johnny Cash was topping the bill again. I also booked a woman called 'Rattlesnake Annie' for the sound of her name as much as anything.

Although I always found that most people could be trusted to keep their word in the business, there were always exceptions. There was a German promoter for instance, called Mike, who I used to work with in Frankfurt. What would happen was that the sponsorship money would come directly to me, and the exhibition money would be paid at the event and I would collect it at the end. The promoter would collect the ticket, programme and merchandise money and then hand my share over to me in a meeting at the end of the evening. Because there was so much cash involved my insurance company insisted that I take a minder to the meeting with me, so I would take a gentle giant called Tony Erdman, who was also a great mate. I would also have Ken Salter, the accountant, and other reliable people with me to pay the artists and to take care of all the other details.

Mike hadn't turned up for the meeting after one festival so Tony went to look for him. He came back saying that he couldn't find him anywhere. It wasn't long before we realized Mike had done a runner with about fifty thousand pounds of my money in German currency. The next morning I had to put the whole entourage of about a hundred people on to a train to Zurich to do another festival and there was no way I could let them all go without me. I also had to take Tony with me for insurance reasons, so I left one of the sound guys to try to track Mike down and recover my money. Eventually, after a lot of digging, we found out he had left his wife, gone off with a young woman and had used some of the cash to purchase a great deal of coke for personal consumption. He had now vanished completely from sight and I was obviously going to need someone other than some poor sound man to take up the trail from there.

I knew a man called John Blower who was very good at finding lost people. John was a friend of mine and I had done him a few favours in the past. He used to manage an British country act called Lynch and Lawson. He had spent about twelve thousand pounds making an album with them, which he then couldn't do anything with. I took the album off him and did a record deal with Don Arden for his Jet Records label, which included Raymond Froggatt, Carl Perkins and a couple of others, and I slipped Lynch and Lawson into the deal, getting John his twelve grand back. So, I knew he would be very happy to return the favour. I rang him and asked him to track missing Mike down. A few weeks later he phoned me from Rome.

'We've got him,' he said, 'but he's knocked all the money out.'

'How do you know he's knocked all the money out?' I asked. 'Maybe he's lying.'

'Well, he's hanging out the window at the moment, so we can be pretty sure there's no money left. What do you want us to do?'

'You'd better pull him back in, John,' I said. 'I may have lost the money, but I don't want to be involved in anything else.'

Sometimes you just have to accept that you win some and you lose some.

East Meets West

In 1974, when the Cold War between the Soviet Union and the West was at its peak, the American State Department approached me via the American embassy in London and asked if I would take some country artists to Russia. Apparently the authorities over there had agreed to allow some performers in, since they saw country as the 'music of the people'.

I took George Hamilton IV over with me. He and I always got on well, which was just as well, since travelling in communist Russia was a test of anyone's patience in those days. You needed to be with someone you could have a laugh with or you would go mad. We were put up at a hotel in Red Square, which was a horrible experience, and the food was equally dreadful wherever we went. The mood of the people was aggressive and gloomy. We went to see Lenin's tomb. It was freezing cold so I had my hands in my pockets, until a soldier hit them hard with the butt of his gun to make me show them. But underneath all the oppression there was still a glimmer of rebellious spirit trying to break through, especially amongst the young. We did one concert at Moscow University and when George started to sing 'Down by the Riverside' the whole audience sang along to lines like 'We'll lay our atom bombs, down by the riverside.' It was an impressive sound.

I went back to the Soviet Union about twelve years later. The communists were still in power but their grip was loosening and business opportunities were starting to show themselves. I had a guy working for me called Carl Lewis who had suggested that I should look East for acts that I might bring over to Britain.

'You're always looking West.' he said. 'After the war there was a big group of entertainers called The Red Army Ensemble who came over to perform and were really good. You should see if they would like to come to the West again.'

I had also had dealings with Czechoslovakia in 1974 when I brought over a group called Country Beat. They were okay, but it was more of a political move as I was invited over to Prague, taking George Hamilton IV and a British band called The Johnny Young Four. The people we had met had made us incredibly welcome, even though they had nothing themselves.

I thought about what Carl had said and decided he was right. It was a market that no one else was looking at, which meant there might well be opportunities that were being overlooked. When I investigated more closely I discovered that the musicians, choirs and dancers of the Red Army Ensemble were working all over the Soviet Empire and the authorities liked the idea of being able to show them off to the West in the same way they had been able to show off their gymnasts and ballet dancers.

When I informed them what I was thinking of doing they asked if I would like to come over as their guest and see for myself what they could do. Remembering how primitive life in the Soviet Union had been on my last visit, I didn't want to have to go too far into the wilderness, so I looked for some venues in their itinerary where I might be able to see them in action around Moscow and Laura said she would like to come too.

This time I was given the full VIP treatment. When we arrived there was a car waiting to greet us at the airport and take us straight to the hotel, where I bumped into Robert Maxwell, the infamous and enormous newspaper mogul and former MP, wandering around the reception area in his trademark baseball cap. He too knew that there were big business opportunities to be found in the East for those who had the nerve to come looking.

'What are you doing here?' he wanted to know when he heard me speaking English.

'I'm booking the Red Army to perform in the West.'

152

'They're very good,' he boomed. 'I know all about them. I was in the army in Berlin. When you get back to England contact me and I will help you. Is there anyone I can help you with while you are here?'

'It's all right, thank you, Mr Maxwell,' I said politely. 'But very kind of you to offer.'

'Don't worry,' he reassured me. 'I like to help young people get on in their careers.'

Even at that stage some instinct told me that this was not a man I would ever want to be indebted to. It wasn't until his mysterious disappearance from his yacht in 1991, however, that we all found out the full extent of his fraudulent activities.

The officials of the Red Army were obviously very keen to impress me. They put a show on just for me in their military barracks with a cast of more than a hundred very talented people. They had even drafted in two guest singers to join them from the Bolshoi Opera. It was a fantastic show, but it went on for hours, far longer than would ever have been acceptable to Western audiences. I asked the organisers if they would mind me spending a few days with them making changes to the show's running time. They were extremely helpful and I managed to cut it down by two hours, tightening the whole thing up dramatically. Happy that I now had an exceptional show on my hands, I returned to Britain and took a big gamble, booking them a major national tour, including a week at the Albert Hall. I also arranged to donate half the proceeds of the opening night to The Heart Foundation, a charity I had been introduced to by a neighbour in Wimbledon called Christina, who had asked me to be on her committee.

At that time Margaret Thatcher and Ronald Reagan were working with President Gorbachev, negotiating the restructuring (perestroika) of Soviet politics and economics. It looked very hopeful that the Cold War would soon be a thing of the past, although nobody then could predict just how dramatically the end would come about and the wall would fall. My press officer suggested that it would be good publicity if Mrs Thatcher could be persuaded to come to the show since the press always reported everything she did.

'You think she'll come?' I asked, not imagining that sitting still for a couple of hours in a theatre would be to the taste of someone who was so famous for her restless energy and lack of patience.

'Let's ask her,' he said. 'What have we got to lose?'

I sent an invitation for the opening night to 10 Downing Street, which, to my surprise, the Prime Minister immediately accepted. I then had to think of how I could make the evening as interesting for her as possible. I had Crystal Gayle, who I happen to think should have been a much bigger star than she eventually was, and Willie Nelson on tour at that time so I asked them to come and be my guests that night as well so that we could make it into an event for her. I had no idea whether she would have any idea who they were or not. I laid on a big reception in one of the rooms at the Albert Hall, feeling extremely nervous about spending time with a woman who had already been dubbed 'The Iron Lady' by the press for good reason.

To my surprise and delight Mrs Thatcher was completely charming from the moment she swept into the room and started shaking hands. She circulated and talked to all the other guests, making an effort to put everyone at ease until the time came for us to go to our seats. The hall was packed to the rafters and from the moment it started it was obvious the audience loved the show and I had a potential hit on my hands.

Mrs Thatcher announced that she wanted to go backstage to meet some of the performers during the interval. She didn't, however, want to go through any back doors – she wanted to be seen walking through the auditorium with all her security people around her. Afterwards I invited more of the performers to another reception backstage and she met them as well, not seeming to be in any hurry to leave and showing an equal interest in everyone. As she was leaving she said she'd had such a nice time she would like Laura and me and the man in charge of the ensemble to come to Number 10 for dinner with her the following week.

Mrs Thatcher had been a complete joy all through the evening, interested in everything that was going on, talking to

154

everyone. The following night Princess Anne was my guest and we were donating the money to The Autistic Society. She was nowhere near as gracious. Virtually the only thing she deigned to say all evening was, 'How long is this going to go on for, then?'

I felt immensely proud as I drove my Bentley into Downing Street a week later. Mrs Thatcher was the perfect hostess, greeting us like old friends and showing us all round the house, bustling ahead of us and opening curtains so we could better appreciate the views out over Horse Guards Parade. I made a mental note of everything that happened so that I could regale Mum with the whole story the next time I saw her.

The fact that Mrs Thatcher had come to the Red Army show was all over the papers and the reviews of the show itself were good so demand for tickets went through the roof. As a result I had to increase the tour to ninety days, which the Russians were very happy about, and by the end of it I'd grossed nearly a million pounds. Word of the tour's success then got round the other Soviet Bloc countries and all the communist governments started contacting me and inviting me over to view the entertainment sections of their armies. Because I was the first to go over there I was the only Western impresario that anyone behind the Iron Curtain really knew. It certainly seemed that mine was the only phone number that was being passed around. I went to see the Poles, the Czechs and the Hungarians.

I took George Hamilton IV with me to Hungary to do some shows, and on another occasion I took Johnny Cash, who I had got back in contact with through the festivals. One evening during George's tour, he and I were having dinner in a hotel overlooking Victory Square where there was a riot brewing up as the crowds stood up to the tanks which had been sent to intimidate them. It was like watching a movie in real life. History was happening before our eyes.

I took Johnny to perform in Czechoslovakia, having agreed to bring one of their bands back to Britain in a reciprocal arrangement. When I arrived at my hotel there I saw a girl waiting in the lobby, but I didn't recognize her so I took no notice. I checked in and went up to my room. A few minutes later there was a knock on the door. When I opened it I found the girl standing there, smiling innocently.

'Mr Conn?' she said.

'Yes?'

'I am with you?'

'What do you mean, you are with me?'

'Yes.' Her smile faltered a little but she didn't give up. No doubt she had had her orders. 'I am your lady. To take care of you.'

'To take care of me?'

'While you are here.'

The penny finally dropped and I thanked her kindly, promising that I would let her know if I needed anything. I had been to the Eastern Bloc enough times by then to know that the rooms would be bugged and that should I misbehave it would be on the record for ever. Any negotiating I might want to do in the future would be severely handicapped if they could threaten to blackmail me.

The Red Army tour was such a success I arranged to bring them over again, and this time there were a couple of singers from the Bolshoi Opera included in the cast. Previously the Bolshoi Ballet's requirements had been handled in Britain by some people called Robert and Vickie Patterson and when they heard what I was doing they thought I was encroaching on their territory. They told me that I couldn't use the word 'Bolshoi' in any of my advertising. In fact, it was only mentioned once in an explanatory leaflet, so I took no notice. They ended up suing me for 'misrepresentation to the public'. I thought it was totally unfair because these were singers from the Bolshoi, nothing to do with the ballet, and it was the Red Army who had hired them in the first place, not me. We ended up in the High Court and there were lots of delays as the Pattersons said they were waiting for someone to arrive from Moscow to speak on their behalf. In the end the judge grew tired of adjourning the case. In his summing up he warned me that I was 'sailing close to the wind' but he still found in my favour and the tour was able to go ahead as planned.

A similar thing happened with an agent and promoter called Derek Block who was touring the Bolshoi Ballet. At the time I was busy doing seven country festivals and a jazz festival and various other tours, but when I was approached by an assistant conductor of the Red Army Ensemble, who had just left the Army and had a concept to bring the Moscow Symphony Orchestra to the West, including six major stars from the Bolshoi Opera Company, I couldn't resist.

The Bolshoi Company is made up of about sixty per cent ballet and forty per cent opera, so the ballet takes precedence in their global marketing plans. Classic FM, the radio station, had just been launched and this conductor had managed to get them interested in the idea. A record company also went along with it and everything seemed to be falling neatly into place, as sometimes happens. We started by recording the orchestra in Moscow, which involved me in spending a fair bit of money. I then booked a major tour to promote the record and when I announced it Derek rang to tell me I couldn't do it because he was bringing the Bolshoi Ballet in at the end of the year.

'It'll take our business away,' he said.

'But this is opera, not ballet,' I tried to reason with him. 'It's a different company and a different clientele.'

He wasn't willing to listen and he persuaded the man in charge of the ballet in Moscow to put pressure on to my singers, threatening to take away their apartments, which were located in the best parts of the city, if they fulfilled their obligations to me in Britain. Four of the singers caved in to the pressure but two stood by their word and agreed to honour their contracts to me. The theatres were booked, the records pressed and the programmes printed. I was totally committed and would lose about a hundred and fifty thousand pounds if I was forced to cancel.

I tried pleading with Derek again, but he wasn't having it, and he issued a press statement saying that I was bringing 'fake Bolshoi opera singers' into the country, which got into the papers just as he intended. I had no option but to cancel after that but I took Derek to court for libel. I was awarded forty thousand pounds in damages, but the case had cost me nearly that much to prepare, so I ended up losing a great deal of money.

The Russians then asked me to bring the Bolshoi Ballet to Britain for another tour when they were doing a production of Les Sylphides, which is a short piece made up of a number of sylphs dancing in the moonlight to the music of Chopin. The male dancer played a poet and it was a role that had once been danced by Nijinsky in Paris and later by Nureyev in London and New York. The prima ballerina of this particular company was getting on a bit, although she was still a great dancer, but she instructed that the lighting should be low in order to flatter her. Because it was meant to be moonlight I didn't notice initially but each night it seemed to be getting darker and by the third night it was so black I could barely make out the dancers. It was only when I asked the lighting director what was going on that I discovered he was under instructions from the leading lady.

'Never mind her,' I told him, 'just turn the lights up so the audience can see the dancing.'

Amongst the many invitations I received from the Eastern Bloc was one from the Russian Navy, asking me to bring them over to perform in the West. They invited me to Sebastopol, which was still a closed city at the time, as their guest and put on a wonderful night for me with their show and a big dinner.

When I returned to Moscow a few years later to negotiate to bring the Red Army back for another tour, which I would eventually do several times, they put on a splendid banquet for me in an ornate gold banqueting room at the Kremlin. It was a great thrill for me to think that my grandfather had had to leave southern Russia all those years before because of the pogroms, and now I was back there, being feted by the army as a guest of honour. There must have been about thirty people round our table, which was loaded with caviar and smoked salmon, including the Minister of Defence. In traditional Russian style, everyone had to make a speech and a toast, followed by a shot of vodka. By the time we were half way round the table I was already finding it hard to stand up straight, but it was still a wonderful feeling to be so appreciated.

'I must own up to you now,' I said as the vodka warmed my courage and it came to my turn to speak. 'I think my grandfather had been conscripted for the Russian Army when he left the country. I feel he is up there now looking down at me and laughing.'

After a moment's silence there was a ripple of confused laughter as the joke was translated and explained and then the glasses were raised once more with a roar of approval. That trip was just before the wall fell and Russia opened up to the West, and if I had only known what was round the corner I would have bought some property in Moscow while it was still worth nothing and by now I'd be up there with the other billionaires. If only it was possible to see into the future.

It was a very different atmosphere to the night that Laura and I went for a banquet at President Carter's White House, after I had been made International Vice President of the Country Music Association. Just like our night at 10 Downing Street, we were taken on a guided tour, and we stayed at the Adams Hotel across the road. We were even allowed to peek into the Oval Office, although we were warned not to step over the threshold. That was another night that Lily wanted to have recounted to her in full detail.

Because they knew that I had handled the Red Army tour, the Chinese Embassy approached me to arrange a tour for their Peking acrobats, who had a phenomenal act, unlike anything we had seen in the West up till then. I booked them into theatres all over England and then I took them across to France and Switzerland. That led to approaches from Korean dancers from South Korea and the Ukrainian State Dance Company. The Ukrainians invited me over to Kiev to see them perform, which was a wonderful experience that not many people from the West had had at that time.

The contrast between the various different parts of my life was what made it so exciting. I arranged a forty-eight performance tour for the Polish Ensemble of the Polish Army in the

159

same year that I toured with Boxcar Willie, a true mix of East and West at a time when the divisions between the two seemed almost unbridgeable.

Miss Dietrich And Jerry Lee

Marlene Dietrich had been a star from long before I was even born, epitomizing European glamour and mystery from the pre-war period. Born in Germany, she was acting on the stage in Berlin in the 1920s and in the early silent films of the period. In 1930 she acted and sang in *The Blue Angel*, which made her a worldwide star, took her to Hollywood and created an iconic image which is still instantly recognizable today, nearly twenty years after her death.

After the war she had made a few more films but spent most of her time touring her one-woman show, singing the cabaret songs that had made her famous, like 'Falling in Love Again,' 'Lili Marlene' and 'The Boys in the Backroom', evoking the smoky, decadent atmosphere of Berlin, which was later the backdrop to the film *Cabaret*. In 1999 the American Film Institute named her the ninth greatest female star of all time and Jean Cocteau was quoted as saying of her, 'Whoever knows her and has been able to experience her has experienced perfection itself.'

In the early seventies Marlene had a press guy looking after her in London called Michael Stackpool, who was sent to see me by Derek Taylor to ask if I would like to handle the British end of her final world tour. She was seventy-five years old by then, but I knew there would still be a lot of people who would be willing to pay to see such a great legend perform live one more time. Apart from anything she had a huge gay following who I was confident would turn out in force to see her. I agreed to handle it and was told that whenever she was in London

Miss Dietrich always liked to stay in the same suite at the Savoy.

'I'll arrange for you to have an account at the hotel,' Michael said. 'Miss Dietrich likes the impresario to do that so the accountant can take care of everything.'

It sounded like some hangover from the Hollywood studio system of the twenties, but I was very happy to humour such a venerable star. I opened the account, took her for dinner and did everything that was expected of me. I was not disappointed – she was totally charming and her mind was as sharp as it had ever been. I booked her in for a three-week season at Wimbledon Theatre and because she had difficulty getting about we put a caravan for her to use as a dressing room on the side of the stage, a bit like on a film set. She'd had a special dress created on top of a sort of thin, latex sheath that fitted exactly to her body, giving her the figure she'd had thirty years before. She sang exactly like she always had, with a full orchestra behind her.

On the second day of rehearsals I could see that everything was going well and since I was just round the corner from home I thought I would slip away and get in a bit of time in my garden. I always found gardening a very therapeutic way to empty my mind of all the business stuff that was constantly buzzing around inside my head. I had changed into my gardening clothes and boots and was pottering happily in the greenhouse when a call came through from the theatre.

Laura took the call and came out to tell me there was some sort of trouble with Marlene and I had better get back down there. Assuming it must be urgent I didn't stop to change back into my work clothes, although I did take off my muddy boots before climbing into the car, and I hurried back down to find her sitting in the caravan, waiting for me. I knocked and she summoned me in, slowly looking me up and down like I was something she had just found on the bottom of her shoe.

'Mr Conn,' she growled. 'You are the impresario. When I am rehearsing in the theatre you will be in the theatre. And the next time you come into my dressing room you will dress properly. Thank you, Mr Conn. Good afternoon.'

162

'Yes, Miss Dietrich.'

I felt about two inches high, like a scolded schoolboy, which I guess was pretty much her intention.

During the time that she was playing at Wimbledon we received a call at the office from the Lord Mayor of Wolver-hampton. I think he might have had to try several times before the girl on the switchboard actually believed he was the genuine article and put him through to me. Finally, however, we were speaking.

'I'd like to have Miss Dietrich come to sing at our civic hall,' he told me.

'That will be a pretty expensive business,' I warned.

'I don't care what it costs,' he assured me. 'I have been a life-long fan. I think she is wonderful.'

'I will have a word with Miss Dietrich this evening,' I promised, 'and I will let you know.'

I duly put the idea to her and to my surprise she agreed to consider it. Getting her to agree, however, was only the first step. Now we had to organise for the entire orchestra to travel with her, as well as the stage-side caravan, her carpet, her food and everything else that she needed to feel comfortable. I repeated my warning to the Lord Mayor that it was going to cost a fortune just for one night.

'I don't care what it costs,' he said again.

The concert happened and Marlene then flew to Canada to continue her farewell tour. She left the Lord Mayor a happy man, but I should think the local rates had to go up the next year as a result.

I did a number of 'final tours' over the years, including Peggy Lee, the jazz singer most famous for her cover version of 'Fever'. Peggy was already seriously ill when she said she wanted to go out on the road one more time and she had to have a respirator at the side of the stage just in order to be able to breathe. She would come off between songs for her air just so that she could keep going.

In 1981 I put on a big 'sixties revival' tour of acts like Lou Christie and Scott McKenzie, who had sung the anthem of the

163

flower power era 'San Francisco (Be Sure To Wear Some Flowers In Your Hair)' and starring a reformed version of The Mamas and the Papas, which was their last big tour together. I did a final tour for the real Temptations, one of Motown's biggest acts, before they all got changed around with new members, and another for Sarah Vaughan and Billy Eckstine. Billy was a real gentleman. Sarah was lovely too, but always coked up. At the end of their last tour, after I had organized a jazz festival and a number of concerts, I hired Morton's Club in Berkeley Square, not far from where I used to hang out at the Astor and Colony clubs as a young man, for a final party for both of them and for Brook Benton. Brook had had a great comeback with the track 'Rainy Night in Georgia' in 1970. The three of them performed with a quartet I had hired into the small hours of the morning and it was one of the most memorable nights of my life. I think it was the last time any of them played in Britain.

Not all the stars were as much of a pleasure to work with. Roberta Flack was always particularly fussy, complaining about everything from the temperature of the champagne in her dressing room to the colour of the bread on her smoked salmon sandwiches, but I had to bite the bullet and try to satisfy all her whims because she was a great singer and she did sell a lot of tickets whenever she went out on the road.

Quite often it wasn't the artists themselves who caused the problems but the people who surrounded them, as I had discovered to my cost with Don Williams. Tammy Wynette, whose records like 'Stand By Your Man' and 'D.I.V.O.R.C.E.' were amongst the biggest selling singles in country music history, was a lovely woman who'd had a very sad life. I'd booked her to headline at the festival and the day before she was due to fly over her manager, who was also her husband at the time, rang me in the middle of the night to say that they weren't coming unless I paid them another ten thousand dollars. I pointed out that we had a contract, but he didn't care, and he wanted it paid before they would get on the plane. I explained that there wasn't time but promised to give them the money when they arrived. I couldn't afford to lose her at that stage, as he well knew.

Another time I went to her house after there had been a kidnap attempt of some sort, and the place was bristling with armed guards on the roof and at the doors. It all seemed to be completely out of her control and I felt very sorry for her. There was a plus side to her husband's devotion as well. On her last trip to England for me she got sick and he took the Concorde to New York and back in a day just to get the drug she needed to keep going.

Showbusiness attracts all sorts of people and there was sometimes a degree of brinkmanship involved in getting paid by some of the hustlers in the business. Johnny Cash was once booked to do a show in Germany, where all the tickets had been sold and we were supposed to be paid before going on stage. Helmut, the guy who was supposed to be giving us the money, kept not showing and his assistant kept telling me 'not to worry', that he had been delayed but would be there 'soon'. He still hadn't shown up at the time the show was due to start so I told Johnny to stay in his dressing room.

The crowd was beginning to become restless and the assistant came backstage to find out what was going wrong. I explained yet again that we were contracted to be paid before Johnny went on.

'But Helmut is coming,' he said, for what seemed like the millionth time.

'Then we'll wait till he gets here,' I said.

Helmut arrived five minutes later, just as the crowd was starting to turn ugly, with the promised cash in his briefcase. It was in local currency rather than the dollars we were supposed to have, but that was fine. He had obviously had to scrape it together at the last minute.

It is perfectly normal for acts to be paid up front, but not usually in cash. The normal method is to set up an escrow account so that the artist knows it is there, but sometimes that is not enough to make them feel safe.

Chuck Berry was big in France as well as Britain and I used to set up shows for him to go on to over there after finishing his touring commitments here. One year he was due to do ten cities over there and on the final night in Britain he called me into his dressing room and informed me that he wanted all his money for the French tour up front and in cash. As he was on about ten thousand dollars a night that was going to be an inconvenient amount of money to raise at such short notice. I tried to reason with him but he wasn't willing to budge. Feeling deeply irritated, and slightly insulted that he didn't trust me after we had already been working together, I rang my bank and asked them to find a hundred thousand dollars for me in cash, but to make sure that there was no denomination bigger than a twenty dollar note. The resulting case full of money was delivered the next day. Taking a security man with me I went backstage and we waited in Chuck's dressing room until he came off stage, when I carefully counted it all out in front of him, not volunteering to give him the briefcase to carry it in. Watching him frantically trying to stuff it into his pockets was worth all the effort.

I heard that he did the same to a promoter in Australia, at a time when they had introduced a withholding tax down there. Chuck thought he could evade the tax by having his fee in cash so he insisted that the promoter found it for him. The promoter didn't want anyone to accuse him of colluding in tax evasion so he tipped off the authorities, who were waiting for Chuck as he walked out to his plane.

'Mr Berry, can we have a minute of your time? Are you going out of Australia with any undeclared currency?'

'No, Sir,' he replied, brazening it out.

'Could you just accompany me into this room, Mr Berry?'

They confiscated the lot.

Jerry Lee Lewis also knew how to work the system in his favour. Whenever I was taking an artist on tour I would always be happy to pay their hotel bills as part of the deal, but not the extras: that was up to them. Jerry never took any notice of that rule and I got a call from the Royal Garden Hotel, where I had booked him in, one day in the late eighties to say that Harrods had just rung to put fifteen hundred pounds worth of his wife's shopping on the hotel bill. The hotel manager wanted to know if I was willing to authorize it. I made it quite clear I wouldn't, that I was paying only for the room.

'You do realize, don't you, Mr Conn, that Mr Lewis has run up a big bill here for extras,' the manager said.

'Like how much?' I asked, experiencing a familiar sinking feeling.

There was a pause while he checked the figure. 'About seven thousand pounds.'

'Well,' I reminded him, 'you have it in writing from me that I'm not paying for it.'

'I'm afraid if he doesn't pay by tomorrow he will have to leave the hotel.'

I said I would get back to him once I had found out what was going on and that evening I heard that Jerry was now refusing to go on stage in Bournemouth because I wasn't willing to pay for his wife's shopping trip to Harrods. The show was at the BICC and was sold out, all two and a half thousand seats. I refused to be blackmailed and the next day Jerry carried out his threat, flying out of Britain without paying the hotel and without completing the tour, leaving me with bills of about forty thousand pounds, which he still hasn't refunded me to this day.

He wasn't the only one to do that. I managed a famous American singer called Guy Mitchell for a few months, but he kept on running up bills and proved to be too eccentric to be worth the effort.

Jerry liked to keep the people around him on their toes. On a tour with him in Switzerland we were all out together after the last night of the show, when I took everyone involved to a nightclub. Jerry called me over to his table where he was sitting with his band members. I was with a couple of the girls who worked for me and we went over together. He was holding a sharp knife.

'Look at this,' he said, putting the blade of the knife into the palm of his hand and starting to squeeze, harder and harder until the blood began to flow, making the girls squeal.

'What did you do that for?' I asked.

'I want you to know how tough I am, Mervyn,' he said, as if that explained anything.

In Monte Carlo we put on a private show for Princess Caroline and before the show started one of the equerries came and asked me if I could persuade Jerry to do a bit longer for the Princess as she was such a fan.

'Of course he will,' I assured the man, although I couldn't even be sure he would come on stage at all if he happened to be in a bad mood. 'He'd love to do it for her.'

Luckily for me Jerry was enjoying himself that night and did an extra fifteen minutes without me even having to ask. At the end of the night the equerry came looking for me to thank me, giving me an envelope, which I slipped into my pocket unopened, intending to look at it later. When I did open it I found a five thousand franc tip to me for extending the show.

By the time I got back to the hotel Jerry had disappeared upstairs and a reporter from the *News of the World* was on the phone to me saying that they had heard he had a room full of hookers. He had always been a controversial figure for the British media, ever since he had married an underage girl who was also a cousin of some sort.

'Can you give us the story on it?' the reporter wanted to know.

I could truthfully say I didn't know anything about it, and I didn't want to know anything either, since I was well aware that his wife was in London waiting for us to come back the following day and might well be reading the British papers.

On another occasion Jerry was playing the Olympia in Paris. He was due to appear next in Oslo when I received a call to tell me the theatre in Oslo had burnt down and there was no point in Jerry coming. I got hold of Malcolm, the company manager, who was with Jerry and told him to keep him in Paris for an extra day and then go straight to Hamburg. Malcolm was pleased by the thought of getting a day off in Paris in the middle of a tour, as you would expect, but he rang back a bit later.

'Jerry won't stay in Paris,' he told me.

'What do you mean?'

'He refuses to stay because he doesn't like the food here.'

'Are you serious?'

'Absolutely. He wants to come back to London.'

'For one day? I can't arrange flights at this short notice.'

'He says he'll arrange his own flight.'

That night Jerry chartered a plane and flew back to London with all his entourage, at my expense.

Another time I was fast asleep when my phone went off in the middle of the night.

'Mervyn?' the voice came shouting down the line. 'Jerry Lee here.'

'What do you want, Jerry Lee?'

'I want to go to a nightclub. Arrange it.'

'Jerry,' I said, fumbling for the clock. 'It's two thirty in the morning.'

'I don't care what time it is. I want to go to a club.'

'Okay, I'll arrange for you to go to the Speakeasy.'

I phoned the club, which a friend of mine was managing at the time, to tell them he was on the way and went back to sleep, confident Jerry would like the club and the club would benefit from having a star turning up unexpectedly. Next day I got a call from my friend.

'Don't do me any more favours like that, Mervyn.'

I didn't even ask what had happened because I could imagine.

On a night at the Royal Garden Hotel, when I was throwing one of the festival banquets, Jerry Lee's entourage stole the piano from the hotel lounge. Somehow they got it into the lift and took it up to his suite for a party. Love him or hate him, you couldn't deny the man was the epitome of the rock-and-roll lifestyle.

★ *Expansions* ★

I was always a mad keen Arsenal fan. When the country festivals were at their height in the late seventies there was a player called Pat Jennings who was a big country fan so I invited him along. Pat played over three hundred games in goal for Arsenal and was in three successive FA Cup finals. He introduced me to another fellow, called Vic Groves, who played for them at the end of the fifties and whose nephew, Perry Groves, played for them in the late eighties. They, in turn, introduced me to Alan Sunderland, who the club had paid nearly a quarter of a million pounds for, Malcolm MacDonald, who had been bought for a third of a million, and George Graham, who had joined the team in the sixties. It was the beginning of the modern age of big money for footballers and I thought I could see opportunities for developing their careers.

I suggested that I could manage them in the same way I did singers, and move them forward in their careers, but at that stage the Club did everything for them, which put a lot of restrictions on what I could do on their behalf. None of them had agents or managers in those days – that was all still to come about twelve years later. If the idea had worked I would have been the first on the scene but I was too early and it was impossible to get anything done. Terry Neill, the ex-Arsenal manager, has been a good friend ever since he was a young player at the club and we tried to organize something together too, but it didn't work out.

With all the travelling to America, the organizing of the festivals, the concerts and the tours, I was trying to juggle too many different things at once and I knew that I needed to hire someone to take over the day-to-day management of the whole operation, leaving me free to do the deals and put on the shows. This was new territory for me because I had always been used to working for myself or in partnerships with other people. I wasn't used to recruiting people and paying them salaries, but I knew I needed a managing director.

The first man I hired was John Burrows, who was working as number three at Howard and Wyndham, a big theatre management and production group of the time. He was a charming chap and he negotiated a good package for himself, including a company Jaguar and a handsome expenses account. What I soon realized was that someone who worked as number three in a big company would have all the chat and the ideas but wouldn't ever be the one making the solid decisions, which was what I needed from him. I was number one in the company but I was very aware that I didn't have the background experience and training for the position of a polished, sophisticated chairman. I'd had a good education but pattern cutting at Regent Street College does not prepare you for that sort of role in life. I had pulled myself up by the bootstraps, approaching every problem and opportunity in the same swashbuckling but creative way, and that had left me with a lot of gaps in my knowledge of how to handle people and situations diplomatically.

Within weeks of John arriving, everyone in the office had been upset, but I decided I needed to wait at least six months to give him a chance to bed himself in. The problem was that he knew all about running theatres but not about putting actual shows together. He was having to learn everything from me as he went along, which was not what I needed. After nine months we decided it wasn't working and parted company. He joined Capital Radio, running all their live shows for years and ended up getting an OBE for it.

It was nearly ten years before I plucked up the courage to try hiring another managing director, by which time the business had grown even bigger and harder for me to oversee on my own. The next guy that I tried was David Griffiths, who was general manager at Wembley Arena was another charming and sophisticated chap who I had liked working and socializing with during my association with Wembley. Part of the reason why I thought it would be a good idea to bring him in was because he said he could bring in a lot of security contracts at rugby matches, which I thought would fit well with the rest of the business.

He was very involved with some upcoming event in China, which he had to sort out before he joined, but if he succeeded in pulling the deal off he promised to bring it into the company. Unfortunately while he was in China the Tiananmen Square massacre happened and whatever his deal was going to be never materialized. The security business also failed to materialize. Like John, he had a generous package, and I took him to New York, Nashville and Los Angeles to introduce him to all my contacts there. In LA we stayed in the Beverly Hills Hotel and met a couple of girls in the Polo Bar one evening. We took them out to dinner and I took one of them back to my room, as was my habit, assuming that David would be discreet. After a few months it became obvious to me that the relationship wasn't going to work out and we needed to call a stop to it. I'd chosen a square peg for a round hole yet again when I probably should have been training up some young guy inhouse. Anyway, for whatever reason, David took his revenge by taking Laura out to lunch and telling her all about the girl in Los Angeles. Laura knew what I was like by then but didn't appreciate hearing it from him.

By 1980 my business had grown so much the offices in Chandos Place were no longer big enough to contain all the people I had to hire. Although they held many happy memories and had been incredibly lucky for me, I had moved into every spare inch of the building and the staff were all falling over one another as they tried to go about their jobs. I was going to have to move on.

Having joined the RAC in Pall Mall with the help of my father-in-law, I often used to walk down there from the office. One day as I strolled across town I noticed a for sale sign on one of the buildings in Orange Street, which runs between the Haymarket and Whitcomb Street. I rang the agents and went to have a look. The vendors were asking for two hundred and seventy five thousand pounds. I had friend, Neal McKay, who was a director at Lazards, who I thought might be able to advise me, and invited him to lunch a few days later at a nearby restaurant called Stones. Over the meal I casually suggested we go round to have a look at the building after we had finished.

'It's a lot of money,' I said doubtfully when we had finished looking over it.

'Let me give you some advice, Mervyn,' Neal said. 'It may sound like a lot of money now, but you won't go wrong buying property in such a central location. You will reap the benefit.'

This was the sort of advice I needed. Having come from a background where everyone was nervous of stretching themselves too far and ending up in financial trouble, and having had a taste of that myself with the restaurant in Hanover Square and the theatre in Palma, I didn't want to do anything that would jeopardize the business I had worked so hard to build up. On the other hand, if I was going to move forward I had to be prepared to take a few calculated risks. On balance this seemed like a sensible thing to do. Most of the people I knew who had invested in property over the years had come out ahead of the game in the end. I decided to take the plunge.

I had a hundred thousand pounds in the company bank accounts so I used that, and borrowed the rest from the Nat West. I went in with an estate agent called Tony Lorenzo helping me with the deal. I had always thought I was pretty good at negotiating, but Tony showed me I still had a lot to learn. We were just about to sign the papers when he stopped the proceedings in a phone call.

'Mervyn doesn't really want to exchange,' he said, which was as much of a surprise to me as it was to the vendors. 'He feels it is a bit too expensive.'

'Our client will reduce the price by ten thousand pounds,' the lawyer at the other end said.

'No,' Tony replied, 'but if they knock it down by fifteen thousand Mervyn would be able to go ahead.'

'Okay,' the lawyer said.

I was amazed. That taught me a lesson in brinkmanship.

It was a huge building with more space than I needed for offices so I turned the basement into a big rehearsal room and dance studio and recruited a woman to run it as a gym. I took on someone else to start an agency division and then put all the various parts of the empire in different rooms. On the top floor I installed a penthouse office and flat for myself and I hired a cook to do lunches so I could entertain people in private without having to go to restaurants every day. It was a pretty impressive set up, even if I say so myself, and I was surprised by how easily it had all come together.

On the corner of Orange Street there was a little greengrocer's shop where the cook and I used to buy supplies for the office lunches. Because of the years I spent working with Dad in his shop I used to like going in and chatting to the guy who owned it.

I was in with him one day when he told me he was a bit sad because he had heard that his landlords were planning to sell the building, which would mean he would have to move his shop after having been there for years and having built up a regular clientele. As I came out and went back to the office with a few fruit and veg items, I got to thinking. Should I buy it? The first building had already proved to be a good investment and I needed to think about building something that would give me a pension when I no longer wanted to be working the whole time (even back then I could see that the traditional pension plans only provided limited potential).

I decided to look into it a bit deeper and found that the building was going for around a hundred thousand pounds, which didn't seem so much now that I was more used to dealing in property. I duly bought the building and the greengrocer was able to keep his shop on until he eventually became ill and had to retire.

Tony Lorenzo, my estate agent friend, was going out with a girl called Stephanie Lawrence, who was a big musical star in the West End at the time, having replaced Marti Webb as Eva Peron in *Evita*. Tony wanted me to handle Stephanie in the same way that I handled people like George Hamilton IV and Slim Whitman. I agreed because they were both such good friends and Laura and I used to go out with them to clubs like Annabel's and Arethusa's, but personal management wasn't a

175

role I was good at. George and Slim were both based in America and didn't make that much of a call on my time, but a West End star like Stephanie needed someone to be on her case all the time, which wasn't part of my nature. We tried it for a couple of months before I suggested that for the sake of our friendship I should pass her on to someone with more experience of day-to-day artist management.

Matt Munro had come to me with a similar proposition around that time. He and I had known each other from the beginning, both of us originating from the same part of London and having friends in common like Don Black. One of his first jobs had been as a bus driver on the number 27 from Highgate to Teddington. The first time I met him properly was when he was on the same bill as Mike and Bernie for a summer season show in Weymouth, which was also where Bernie met his wife, Siggy, who was dancing in the same show. I met Matt again in a hotel in Palm Springs when I was taking a weekend out from the hurly burly of Los Angeles and spent a good evening playing poker with him and his wife. I was a big admirer of his singing and he was a huge international star by the time he asked me to manage him, having sold over a hundred million records. I told him I would be happy to do the job as long as he realized that I wasn't the sort of guy who wanted to be constantly rung up at all hours of the day with minor problems and complaints. I knew that he wouldn't be a difficult artist and we drew up all the papers just before he discovered he had cancer. He was dead within a few months, which was a great sadness for everyone who knew him.

I also managed Lonnie Donegan for the last few years of his career. Lonnie was another one who I knew well enough to be able to explain that I was only going to be willing to do the deals and negotiating for him, but that I wouldn't be willing to do any 'babysitting'. Lonnie was Britain's biggest recording star before The Beatles changed everything. His style of skiffle was said to have influenced everything that came afterwards. He best remembered for comedy songs like 'My Old Man's a Dustman' and 'Does Your Chewing Gum Lose its Flavour (On the Bedpost Overnight)?' People sometimes forget his other work, like the enormous hit he had with a country song called 'Rock Island Line'.

Laura and I were out at dinner one night with Tony and Stephanie, talking about Orange Street, and Tony suddenly laughed.

'I know what you're up to, Mervyn,' he said.

'Yeah?' I said, curious as to what he was thinking. 'You tell me what I'm up to then.'

'You've got your offices and now you've bought that building on the corner. You're going to buy all the others in between and do a development, aren't you?'

'How did you know that, Tony?' I said, although the idea had never even occurred to me – until that moment.

'He came up with a bloody good idea there,' I said to Laura as we were driving home.

'Do you really want to get involved in all that aggravation?' she asked, perfectly reasonably.

'No,' I said, 'not really.' But of course I did.

Over the next few weeks I talked to the guy who had a lease on the building next door, which was owned by the Prudential, and he agreed that in principle he would sell me his lease if I bought the freehold of the building. I then went to the Pru and opened negotiations. The next building after that had an Italian restaurant on the ground floor, a gay club in the basement and three hookers working from the rooms upstairs. The final building in the street was smaller. By this time it was 1985 and property prices were rising very fast. One by one I managed to do deals with each of the owners. The guy in the Italian restaurant owned his whole building and, like Tony, worked out what I was up to. Every time I went to him he wanted more money, blaming his 'uncle' in Sicily for forcing him to increase his asking price.

'Why don't you explain to your uncle', I said eventually, 'that I am going to be pulling down all the other buildings in the street. For three years there is going to be nothing but dust and scaffolding all around your restaurant. Or we could come to a fair agreement for the freehold.'

He really upped the price at that stage, demanding it in lira at a fixed rate, knowing I didn't have any choice but to pay him if I wanted to go ahead. By this stage I had spent over two million pounds of the Nat West's money and I had no choice but to keep going. We did the deal.

There was one more building I wanted in order to complete my property package. It was round the corner in Whitcomb Street, and it came up for sale. Someone I had been working with told the owner that if they doubled the price I would still have to pay it. So they took his advice and I had no option but to cough up.

By 1988 I was ready to start work and I had a plan drawn up for knocking all the buildings down and putting up something new, which I submitted to Westminster Council for planning permission. I didn't actually want to do the work myself because I knew that I would not be a good builder.

Once permission had been granted I put the whole project on the market. One of the most serious bidders was Taylor Woodrow, the construction giant, and there was another bidder offering a quarter of a million pounds more. The property market was going at full speed at that time but my instincts told me that it might be overheating and that I should guard against being greedy. I wanted to do a deal with someone who had a reputation and who I knew had the muscle to pull the deal off, so I accepted Taylor Woodrow's offer, although they chipped me down a hundred thousand at the last minute of the negotiations, just like Tony had done on my behalf before. At three o'clock in the morning we finally reached an agreement and signed. I paid off the bank's loans and was left with a couple of million pounds' profit to put towards my pension fund.

Six weeks later the whole property market collapsed. Interest rates soared and people were going bust all over the place. I bought a restaurant, flats and a house in Clapham, an office and two flats in Wimbledon. Just as I had been too early for the boom in managing the careers of footballers, I was almost too late to profit from the property boom. Timing, as always, is everything.

Other Avenues

I moved the office for a while to Whitcomb Street and then rented a building in Conduit Street, right in the heart of Mayfair between Bond Street and Regent Street, close to where I had got my first job in fashion all those years before at Le Chasse. I was there a few years and finally decided it made no sense to be commuting in and out of the West End all the time and paying top-end rent, so I bought another office block in Wimbledon and moved the whole operation closer to home.

Through living in Wimbledon I became very friendly with an enormously successful property developer called Peter Beckwith, whose younger daughter went to school with my daughter, Scarlett. (His older daughter is the well-known society girl Tamara Beckwith). Peter was very involved with The Autistic Society and I joined the committee, organising all their cabarets and shows as well as contributing. I became involved in the same way with Nightingale House, a Jewish retirement home, raising money and arranging their open days and events and persuading people like Jimmy Tarbuck to go there. Peter proved himself to be a stalwart friend, standing by me when I needed support after an employee made false accusations about me, which ended up all over the front pages of the papers. Even though I won the case on appeal the story did my reputation a lot of harm at the time. I had been tipped off by Downing Street that I was up for a knighthood and all that disappeared because mud sticks, even if you have been found innocent by the courts. Tainted by this false accusation I found I was out of the Hurlingham Club and out of my livery company. It had been like a nightmare but Peter went out of his way to be more than a good friend at a very traumatic time for me.

Peter has a brother, Sir John Beckwith, who is also his business partner. After making a fortune in the property business the two of them became involved with showbusiness, buying into a theatre group and a company that owned advertising sites around cricket pitches and a plot that included an ice rink. When they took over the Ambassador Theatre Group Peter offered me a part of the group for a quarter of a million pounds, which I turned down. Thinking back now, I probably should have accepted that offer, as I got on so well with him and they have become one of the biggest theatrical groups in the country (now they even own Wembley Arena, the scene of all my festivals). But at the time I felt I had enough on my plate and live theatres didn't seem to be doing that well.

They then decided they would like to buy my company out, keeping me on to run the entertainment division that they were setting up within their group. I thought that would be an enjoyable idea and we started negotiations. I had often flirted with the idea of joining forces with other entrepreneurs. Harold Davison had suggested it as long ago as the sixties. Harold used to organize Sinatra's tours and married the singer Marion Ryan, whose name was strongly linked with Sinatra and who was the mother of Paul and Barry Ryan, twin brothers who became big pop stars in the sixties. Their biggest hit together was the melodramatic and heavily orchestrated 'Eloise', which Paul wrote and Barry sung and which sold about three million copies.

Harold made the suggestion about us going into partnership over a lunch and I promised to think about it, but I always liked being my own boss. Harold moved out of showbusiness eventually and went back to the States to make another fortune in supermarkets. There had been a lot of approaches like that but I had always shied away. The only person I had ever worked successfully in partnership with was Joe Collins. There were numerous meetings with the Beckwiths and I thought this time I might take the plunge, but in the end I didn't.

180

Another company in their group approached me later about organizing advertising sites at racecourses. I still didn't want to get into bed with anything to do with Sir John, however remotely, but I agreed to take on a consultancy role for a fee of twenty five thousand pounds as that seemed to put enough distance between us. The managing director of the company was in Australia at the time and told me to go into the office to collect ten thousand pounds on account and promised to pay the balance on his return. The cheque was waiting for me as promised. I went to some meetings and started the work.

When the managing director came back from Australia and I reminded him of his agreement to pay the balance he told me that Sir John wanted to see me because he wanted to 'broaden the base' of the situation. I asked if we could just settle the fee first, explaining that I wasn't going to attend any more meetings until the balance was paid. It was becoming increasingly obvious to me that they didn't intend to pay, so I wrote to Sir John and asked him to send the money to Cancer Research. I have no idea if that ever happened. Sometimes you just have to let things go.

I was approached at one time by the director of another company that owned about twenty major racecourses. They wanted to broaden the base of their business by hosting concerts at the courses. I was introduced to David Hillyard, who was the Managing Director of Racecourse Holdings, which owned eight or nine major courses. The introduction was set up by Major General Guy Watkins, the last in a line of British former army officers to run the Royal Hong Kong Jockey Club. I spent four days with him in Hong Kong. Both our sons went to Charterhouse, and we are still very friendly. I had an idea to put concerts on at racetracks after racing events and spent several weeks travelling all over the country visiting various courses and the people who ran them, also having many meetings with David and his team, before laying the whole plan out to them and telling them how it could work. In the end they said no, but took the ideas and set things up in-house without me. Again, I just had to chalk it up to experience. Concerts have, in the past decade or so, become a big item at racecourses, and this is an area that is getting bigger and bigger.

Sometimes it can be something very personal that triggers a decision that in hindsight looks illogical. There was one deal I was about to do once that would have made me about a million and a half on the spot and led on to great things.

'You know, Mervyn,' the guy offering the deal said, 'there are a lot of Jews in this business.'

'Yeah?' I replied cautiously, my guard suddenly going up, wondering where he was going with this.'

'Well,' he went on. 'We don't operate like them.'

I didn't rise to the bait but I did walk away from the deal. It was just a casual comment on his part but it raised all sorts of feelings inside me that I thought I had buried, making me feel very uncomfortable. It's shocking how deep feelings instilled in childhood can run. It was the first time I had been made to feel different just because I was Jewish since I was a young boy during the war, told to sit outside school assembly. I never mentioned the matter to the man himself at the time. I now know that I missed an opportunity to get to the next level of the business world. Maybe I was being too sensitive, but none of us can help the way we feel about things – we are all the products of our own past experiences.

The great advantage of being your own boss is that you can follow your own interests when it comes to choosing what to do and what to drop. Following my own passions, I put on two big jazz festivals, for instance, in conjunction with Granada Television, one at the City Hall in Sheffield and one at the Free Trade Hall in Manchester. Silk Cut sponsored one of them with artists like Peggy Lee, Brook Benton, Ramsey Lewis, the Woody Herman Orchestra, Sarah Vaughan, Billy Eckstine and Stan Getz. Stan was one of the best saxophone players I ever heard but he was a handful, always turning up late and totally unworried by anything. Despite everything he put me through, however, we got on very well together.

Talking of 'handfuls', I took Nina Simone on tour once. She was doing the Barbican Theatre and everything was going well in the first half of the show so Tony Lewis (the same guy that I had done the PJ Proby tour with) and I decided it would be safe for us to go and get some supper while she finished. What we didn't realize as we sat chatting over our food was that during the interval Nina had gone to her dressing room and shot up with some drug or other, which had made her very cantankerous. Instead of going back on stage and singing she started having a political argument with the audience. The theatre manager ran to the restaurant to fetch us because the whole place was in uproar. There was no chance of saving the show. All we could do was bundle her out the back of the theatre into a waiting limo. She had done enough of the show for us not to have to give refunds but I think the Barbican did agree to pay some of the more vociferous complainants as they didn't want any further trouble. Nina had been a civil rights activist when she was young and also had problems with depression, which, along with drugs, created a lethal cocktail.

In 1991 I called a halt to the country festival for a number of different reasons. There was a recession going on to start with, then there were problems with tobacco sponsorship as the government tightened up on what the companies were allowed to do in the way of promotion. After twenty-two years I felt that the concept had run its course. I organised a good final lineup, which included Johnny Cash, Crystal Gale and Willie Nelson. I would have liked to have found someone else to hand it on to, but it had become like a huge military operation and I hadn't been able to find anyone else who was able to hold all the details of it in their head in the way I did. I guess it had become too much for one man to handle.

The country music establishment had treated me with so much respect in Nashville over the years, making me a Freeman of the city, just as I am of London after my father-in-law introduced me into his livery company, that I think perhaps I got carried away with my own importance a bit and perhaps I was too mouthy on one or two occasions. I had a lot of power because of the television and radio coverage of the Wembley festivals and it is always important to remember when you are at the top that you may soon be on the way down again.

The Country Music Association used to hold meetings in different cities all over the world and at one in Acapulco the chair was taken by a very powerful woman called Frances Preston, who was head of BMI, a giant in the music publishing business. Each year they liked to do something special and the committee would discuss and agree what it should be at that meeting. At that time Midem, the music exhibition in Cannes, was one of the biggest events of the year and a very good marketplace to sell records and tapes or to present something new and get exposure to the global music industry. It was a place where millions of pounds worth of business got done every year. I had been taking a booth there every January since long before my involvement with country so I knew all about it. The business would be done during the day and in the evenings they would put on gala concerts.

'I think we should go down to Midem next year', Frances announced, 'with a country music ballet.'

'Jim Halsey tried going to Midem last year,' I said, without thinking, 'putting on a country extravaganza, and it fell on its face. The timing was all wrong and the Europeans aren't interested. I think it would be the wrong time to do it again.'

I should never have opened my mouth because as we came out of the meeting a furious-looking Frances beckoned me over.

'Don't ever go against anything I say in the meeting again,' she growled.

The following October I was off the CMA board and I had learnt a good lesson about American business politics. It is always better to keep your opinions to yourself, even if you are right. Frances got to take her show to Cannes just as she wanted, and it failed miserably just as I had known it would. The fact that I had spoken out of turn, even though I was right, was more evidence of my own lack of sophistication when it came to board room tactics.

I had been involved with virtually every aspect of live enter-tainment over the years, from pop tours to pantomime, from the Bolshoi to the country festivals, and am still being offered new opportunities, most recently with a new TV channel called Vintage, who I will be working with a lot. (You can't keep an old dog down!) I also devised a few shows myself that got to the West End. I devised *The Patsy Cline Story*, with the scenes linked together on stage by George Hamilton IV, because he had actually worked with Patsy in the past. The show did five national tours and a period in the West End at the Whitehall Theatre. On the West End opening night I booked a club in Soho for the after party, inviting lots of celebrities like Olivia Newton John, Cilla Black and Jimmy Tarbuck. My mother loved those West End openings, and was always the life and soul of the parties afterwards. Everyone would make a fuss of her wherever we went.

'Anything we can get for you, Mrs. Conn?' they would ask, buzzing around her like flies.

'Just bring me a toy boy,' she would joke almost every time, until that Patsy Cline opening night when the club manager where we were throwing the party took her seriously and a good-looking young man turned up at her table an hour or two later, introducing himself as her man for the evening. She kept her cool, despite going a little pale, and suggested to him that he should wait outside for her. She didn't make that joke quite as often after that.

Mum always enjoyed the trappings of success. I met up with her and Dad in Los Angeles one time, when I was staying in a bungalow at the glamorous Beverly Hills Hotel, which was the most famous Hollywood hotel in the world and the place where I always stayed when I went there. I then had to leave early for some reason so I suggested that they took over the bungalow for a week. Mum never stopped talking about that.

I followed the Patsy Cline show up with, *The Tammy Wynette Story*. Getting the rights to Tammy's songs in order to do a show after she died was hard because the estate was in a mess, with people disputing who owned what. I had a Scottish friend called Bill Martin, who had written 'Puppet on a String'

185

with his partner, Phil Coulter, which was the song Sandie Shaw won the Eurovision Song Contest with in 1967. They also wrote 'Congratulations' for Cliff Richard the following year, which finished second. We went to Ascot with Bill and as we sat around drinking champagne I was saying that I was having difficulty getting the Tammy Wynette deal sorted.

'I know the Managing Director of EMI,' Bill said airily, 'just leave it with me, Mervyn. I'll get that sorted for you.'

'That's very nice of you, Bill,' I said. I should have known better, having been to a million dinner parties where people boast about all sorts of things they can do for you, most of which never happen.

Bill phoned up a couple of days later saying he was going to Bromley for something or other.

'I'm coming through Wimbledon,' he told me, 'can I drop in to see you?'

He came into the office, chatting away, still promising to sort out the publishing for me.

'What's in it for me?' he asked eventually.

'What do you mean?' I was taken aback. I thought this was a friend doing me a favour, dropping a word in someone's ear. 'How about a case of champagne?'

'I'm not doing this for a joke,' he said indignantly. 'I'm in business.'

'You never mentioned that,' I said. 'What is it you want, Bill? A couple of grand?'

'No,' he said, 'I want a percentage.'

'A percentage of the show for one introduction? Are you crazy? I don't even know what I'm going to be paying for the publishing, let alone the artists. I wouldn't know what the percentage would be of!'

'I'm not here for my health,' he said, and flounced out.

When I told my accountant the story he was equally surprised but suggested I should offer him a quarter of a per cent. I rang Bill later that day to make the offer but he wasn't there and the more I thought about it the more I thought I should sort this out myself. I remembered a charming guy called Al Gallico who lived in Los Angeles and was on the board of

Columbia Music, who controlled the publishing of Tammy Wynette and others. We had been exchanging Christmas cards for years so I got his number and rang that evening. I told him my problem.

'You rang at the right time, Mervyn,' he said, 'because I'm going to New York tomorrow. Leave it to me. I'll square it away and give you a call.'

A few days later he rang while I was still in bed. 'Hi, Merv,' he said. 'It's all squared away, you can go ahead and do the show.'

'That's great, Al. Thanks. What have I got to give you?'

'Next time I come to London', he drawled, 'you can buy me a dinner.'

Some people just know how things should be done.

When it was announced that I was producing the show, Rose-Marie, the Irish singer I had managed many years before, rang and said she would like to play the part of Tammy.

'You'll have to audition just like the other girls,' I warned her. 'I can't ride above the director and his team.'

She understood, so I arranged for her to have a private audition and she brought her own pianist. She was going to sing 'Stand By Your Man', which is a very hard song because of the high note. She had a lot of trouble reaching it and the team decided she wasn't quite right for the part. The show went on and did nearly as good business as Patsy Cline.

I wanted to put on a revival of *The Desert Song* and I approached Topol, the famous Israeli actor who was a big West End star at the time in *Fiddler on the Roof*, to play the lead. We got very friendly, but when he read the script and saw that I was asking him to play an Arab he declined.

I also thought up a children's show about Enid Blyton's *Famous Five* stories. I would hire writers to produce the scripts and then take them into production.

I toured a production of *Annie* with my daughter Scarlett, who had been at Arts Ed drama school, as one of the three girls in the lead role. I hadn't insisted that the director, Peter Walker, hire her, but I suggested we went to Arts Ed and looked for all three of the girls we needed. It was his decision to make

Scarlett his first choice, which I was very happy about. Because the girls were only twelve or thirteen years old they weren't allowed to do every performance and we had to make sure they continued their schooling, but we were still able to tour the production round the country for three years. Bill Maynard played Daddy Warbucks. It was a huge success and I remember watching Scarlett's final performance from the circle of the Theatre Royal Norwich with tears running down my cheeks, knowing that the experience was over and I wouldn't see my little girl playing Orphan Annie again.

Peter Walker was a lovely man and a great director. It was a tragedy when he was murdered a few years later by a man he had picked up and taken back to his flat.

After finishing at Arts Ed, Scarlett went on to work on the cruise liners as a singer and dancer. I wanted to put on *Gigi* with the producer Bill Kenwright with Scarlett in the lead. Bill told me I couldn't just do that because she was my daughter and that she had to audition like anyone else. He was completely right, but I didn't like being told so at the time.

The initial idea for putting on an all-black musical came from Johnny Worthy, the young black guy who had directed *The Patsy Cline Story* for me. I suggested we set it in the Apollo Theatre in Harlem, where I first saw James Brown perform all those years ago, and I suggested that he and I should go across to New York to hold auditions and so he could see the Apollo for himself.

Everyone at the theatre was very friendly and excited by the idea. We held some auditions in New York but, surprisingly, we weren't that impressed with the standard of the performers, so we came back to Britain and held more auditions. Eventually we found the talent we needed. There was also a part for a black girl who looked white, which I thought Scarlett would be good for. She had been in a show about Elvis, which Bill Kenwright had put on in the West End, with Shakin' Stevens and PJ Proby playing the older Elvis and another young actor playing him as a boy. The 'young Elvis' was soon going out with Scarlett. We were starting to do some publicity for the show and the fact that Scarlett and I were father and daughter was interesting the journalists. Esther Rantzen asked if we would go on her show to do a feature about fathers and daughters in showbusiness. I thought that would be brilliant publicity for the show, but 'young Elvis' persuaded Scarlett that this wouldn't be good publicity for her, that she should be a star in her own right. Since I had gone to a fair bit of trouble to get the whole show up and running with her included I was seething, but Laura kept imploring me not to say anything, wanting to keep the peace in the family.

In the end the show ran for eighteen weeks but it didn't take off in quite the way I had hoped and still believe it should have done. Later Scarlett helped me to direct another musical called *Queens of Country*, about Tammy Wynette, Dolly Parton and Patsy Cline, imaging them all starring on the same bill. The show did quite well, although I never took it to the West End. She also appeared in *Cats*.

While I was putting on a Slim Whitman concert at the Fairfield Halls in Croydon in 1998 I heard some music coming from a room downstairs. I wandered down to investigate and found a room full of line dancers having a class. *Riverdance*, Michael Flatley's Irish tap dancing show, which had first come to the attention of mass audiences when they performed during the interval in the Eurovision Song Contest in 1994, was doing well in the West End by then and this seemed like a good idea, which would also fit in with the country market that I knew so well. I met the teacher to pick his brains.

'Does anyone run a national competition to find the best line dancers in the country?' I asked.

'It would be a bit of a mammoth task to travel all over the country doing something like that,' he said.

'Not for me,' I replied. 'We could do this and we could make a DVD of you doing your class as well.'

We agreed to give it a go. I set up a company called Richmond Entertainment and began to organize the whole thing. I advertised it in the country music and line dancing magazines and we ran eighty heats all round the country, hiring teachers from the local line dancing clubs to be judges, sending our star teacher out to judge the more important ones, with me dropping in now and again to see how it was all going. There was a lot of radio coverage and articles and media buzz. There would also be a demonstration team at each venue too to make it more of a show, although it was always the participants who were the main attraction. We then had regional semi-finals in big venues like the Hammersmith Palais in London. The finals were held at Wembley and six thousand people turned up to support their friends and relatives. Round the outside I put up exhibition stands just like I had at the country festivals. We did it for two years before the popularity of line dancing began to wane with the public.

Paul Raymond and I crossed paths again near the end of his life when a friend of mine called Ben de Haan, who went on to open a string of lap dancing clubs, was looking for a premises in the West End. I had heard that Paul was thinking about selling his famous Revue Bar site so I introduced them. Ben was very grateful and promised that we could be partners in anything that resulted from the introduction. At that stage the whole concept of lap dancing was newly imported from America and I didn't really understand what the clubs were going to be about. In the end Paul, who was always a very tough businessman, was asking for so much money that the deal could never have gone ahead. Ben opened a place in Hammersmith called Secrets instead, which immediately boomed, but I wasn't in the picture.

Seeing the way that lap dancing has developed I am relieved not to have got involved. I have always loved the world of clubs but right from the beginning, when I set up Romano's, I have tried to get away from the sleazier aspects of the whole thing. I am not a prude by any means, but I believe a club can have a sexy and glamorous atmosphere without actually resorting to that sort of thing. Things have moved on a long way with regard to nudity and the displaying of women's bodies since Joe turned down Paul's offer of a partnership in the Revue Bar, but in many ways they have also stayed much the same. There is not that great a difference between the lap dancing clubs of today and the hostess bars of the fifties, one of which led to the Profumo affair, which was turned into the film *Scandal* and which brought down the Conservative government in the sixties. John Profumo, then Secretary of State for War, first met Christine Keeler in a Soho drinking club called Murrays.

the same. There is not that great a difference between the lay-
... of the clergy and the ... laymen of the ... state of
which he is the ... Perhaps a few people who ... up to the dig-
... as soon as when brought up to the ... a few ecclesiastical
in the states ... for a ... and to the ... of these the Way
and they become judges for a ... to ... with called
bishops.

★ Lilys ★

Laura and I were married for thirty years. Being in showbusiness, having a larger than average amount of ego and having women throwing themselves at me all the time, I have to admit there were times when I let Laura down, but I was always very careful not to become too involved emotionally with anyone else. I never wanted to do anything that would damage my marriage or my family. I understand that there are many people, particularly women, who will not believe it is acceptable ever to be unfaithful to a partner, and I also understand that there is nothing I can say that will make my womanizing seem acceptable to them. I loved Laura and the children above everything else, but I didn't always find myself able to resist temptation when it was offered. I would eventually have to pay the price.

Despite the pressures of my work I think we still managed to provide a happy family life for the children when they were growing up. Laura unquestionably did a brilliant job as a mother and a wife and she very seldom made a big fuss about my behaviour.

As well as expanding the house in Wimbledon to cater for our increasing needs, I also bought a plot of land on the beach at Dymchurch and built a house for family holidays, which we would go down to every summer. They'd stay for a couple of months during school holidays and I would join them at weekends. One year I thought perhaps we were getting into a rut and needed a change, so I booked us all to take the train down to Nice, but the kids all burst into tears at the prospect of missing Dymchurch. We stayed down on the Riviera for three weeks and they ran up a beach bill of four thousand pounds for all their lunches and drinks, which taught me a lesson.

Although Laura wasn't Jewish, and although my parents had always been pretty relaxed about things to do with religion, I found I did want the children to be brought up in the Jewish tradition. Laura was happy to go along with it and I asked Rabbi Lionel Blue, who is famous for doing 'Thought for the Day' on Radio Two and for being the first openly gay rabbi in Britain, to convert them. Even when they were at boarding schools Dad would drive over every Sunday to collect them and bring them out for their Hebrew classes.

Oliver, our first child, always seemed to feel the responsibility of being the eldest keenly, even though there was only six years between any of the children. He also seemed to feel he had to prove himself to me all the time, which he never needed to do. He went to Charterhouse and then Bristol University and is married now to Jessica, and they have recently produced a granddaughter for me, Kitty.

Scarlett, the next in line, was a real daddy's girl when she was young and looked as if she would be the one who would follow my interests into showbusiness, but after the first few years in the business she seemed to lose the drive that everyone in the industry needs if they want to succeed. She too is married now, to Simon, with two children, Sophia and Edith. They live in Geneva on the French side of the city.

Joseph came next and was a great sportsman as a boy. He went to Charterhouse too, but he wasn't academic like Oliver. I got him a job at the Arsenal Football Club but he moved on to a company that duly went out of business. He is now doing a psychology course and we have grown to be good friends, often playing golf together. He is still great at sport and is one of the star batsmen on Sir Tim Rice's cricket team.

Charity was our fourth child together and was very bright. She became an estate agent with Foxtons and ended up being very successful. She is now married to David and they have two children, Chloe and Arthur. Since the children have grown a little more independent she has gone back to work at Savills.

It seemed to me that Laura and I had been very successful at creating a happy family, which was one of the reasons why it was such a shock to find out that she was having an affair. When I found out it felt like my whole world had fallen to pieces; all the certainties suddenly whipped out from under me. I guess many people would think that I had it coming for my misdemeanours towards Laura over the years, but that didn't make it any less of a shock or lessen the pain. Things were intolerable and I suggested we should have a separation for a while.

'I don't want a separation,' Laura said. 'I want a divorce.'

'We've been married for thirty years,' I tried to reason with her. 'Don't you think we should try to work something out?'

But she was adamant and went to a serious lawyer to set the ball rolling. It seemed she couldn't be dissuaded. My mother died during that time, having reached the fabulous age of ninety-nine, and even though her mind had been wandering a great deal towards the end, I felt I had lost my oldest and greatest friend.

I had reached an age where there were very few people left who shared my early memories. Mike and Bernie's act had broken up acrimoniously at the end of the seventies after they and their wives all opened a hotel together, and Mike had gone off to America. Bernie had worked quite well as a solo act, getting himself a large St Bernard dog called Schnorbitz as a stooge. He also appeared on stage with Leslie Crowther playing Bud Flanagan, the old music hall star in *Underneath the Arches*. He was asked to host several television shows before he died in 1991 of stomach cancer. So many of the people I grew up with are now dead, but I don't really feel any different from how I did forty years ago. I keep myself fit and play a lot of golf with all my friends at Coombe Hill Golf Club.

A couple of years after the marriage ended I was shopping in Tesco and the girl on the till was very friendly. A few weeks later I found myself on her till again and she was equally friendly.

195

'You wouldn't like to come out for a drink, would you?' I asked, expecting to get a polite refusal.

'Yes I'd love to,' she said.

Her name was Nicola and she was in her late thirties. We started to go out together quite regularly and became lovers. Because Nicola had never fallen pregnant in the past we didn't take any precautions and when she was forty-two years old she discovered she was pregnant. By that time I loved her very much and although I was surprised by the news I found I was really looking forward to the thought of a new baby. I was seventy-two years old by then and Nicola, assuming I wouldn't want any more children, didn't tell me to start with. Eventually, of course, it was hard to miss and I asked her outright what was going on. She still didn't tell me but the next day she came back with her mother and told me the truth – that she was pregnant with a little girl and that she had decided to call her Lily. At that moment it seemed like a sign of some sort from my mother, almost as if she was coming back into my life in another body. I felt deeply moved at the thought of this new arrival and suddenly wanted to have her in my life more than anything else.

When Nicola turned up at my golf club with newly born Lily, Jimmy Tarbuck couldn't resist toasting me as 'father of the year' at the next opportunity, comparing me to Charlie Chaplin, who had his last child at about the same age as I am now.

The newly arrived Lily entirely captured my heart. She was a true 'love child'. We made up and Nicola came to spend Christmas day with me, bringing her mother as well as Lily, and I suggested we went on holiday to Barbados. Lily was an absolute delight on the trip but my relationship with Nicola was quite strained. When we got back to England I went to get a copy of Lily's birth certificate and discovered that Nicola had left the father's name blank, which I found more hurtful than I would have expected. Then the lawyer's letters started to fly back and forth and they put freezing orders on all my properties.

It wasn't till the following Christmas that the two of us managed to sit down together, without any lawyers, and find an agreement that both of us think is fair. Lily is such a joy I don't want anything to spoil our time together and I would like her and Nicola to move in with me. Understandably, Nicola is uncomfortable about living in a house that was Laura's, so perhaps once I have sold and moved it will be possible for us to be together as a family unit. She still works at Tesco and we have been on several more holidays with Lily, which have worked well. I still love her and have asked her to marry me many times, but she always sidetracks the question. I pride myself on understanding women better than most men, but they are still a mystery to me.

In a perfect world my little Lily would be able to live with her Mummy and her Daddy, wake up and have breakfast with me each day and, until she starts school, spend her days with me. I missed so much of the growing-up years with my other children when I was busy building the business, and I know that even if I live to be ninety Lily will only have her Daddy around for a limited amount of time. At my age time is very precious and I know that I will not be around when my Lily becomes a woman so I am anxious to spend as much time as I possibly can with her while I am still here, even if it means I have to squabble with Nicola about technical things like custody and access in order to make it happen.

When I am playing with Lily in the Wendy house in the garden and she is bossing me around, it almost feels like my mother is there with me again. She has so many of the same ways even now. Things are not straightforward at the moment, but I hope and pray that this will change over the years that I have left to spend with her. I want her to know that as long as I am alive I will always be there for her.

I find myself thinking more and more about my mother, the first Lily in my life, and my father. I feel that their legacy lives on in their six grandchildren, Damien, Oliver, Scarlett, Joseph, Charity and Lily, and also in their great grandchildren, Sophia, Chloe, Edith, Arthur, Luke and Kitty. Dad's quiet influence is still with me today, making me compulsively neat and ordered in everything I do, unable to tolerate any sort of mess around me. When he died in the 1990s I found an old scrapbook amongst his possessions, which I had never seen before. It was titled 'The One and Only Mervyn Conn' and it was full of all my cuttings and souvenirs of all my achievements. Although I had never been in any doubt about how proud Mum was and how much she enjoyed my every success, I'd had no idea he was compiling such a thing and I was deeply moved. I always knew that I had their total support in anything I wanted to do in life and knowing something like that gave me the confidence I needed to go out into the world and have a go. I hope I have been able to do the same for my own children.

★ Epilogue ★

Thinking back over the last three quarters of a century as I have been, I realize just how many changes I have lived through and how different life in Britain is now from when I first started out, and even more markedly in the hundred years between the birth of Lily, my mother, and Lily, my daughter.

I'm not sure that anyone coming into showbusiness today would be able to follow the same path as I did – the world has changed too much for that. We are churning out a lot of talented young people from the universities and colleges, as well as from all the talent and reality shows. But talented in what, exactly? Everyone expects to get success quickly, but very few people know how to build companies that make money, and on top of that people now have very little chance of getting money from a bank, but without having a few quid to go and do something, you can't move. To be an entrepreneur a young person has to find their way round a whole different obstacle course.

My parents came from a world of travelling circuses and market stalls. A world where everyone had to look after themselves and their own families or face the consequences. But in my lifetime I saw the creation of amazing institutions like the welfare state and the National Health Service, and the arrival of a technological revolution, which started with the introduction of televisions and telephones into every home and now has every individual able to download and listen to or watch any performer they choose whenever they want.

One of the side effects of both these paths, particularly in Europe, is that as a society we are now stifled in red tape every time we try to do something. There are endless forms to be filled in, CVs to be compiled, applications to be made, permissions to be sought out. On top of that, young people are loaded down with debt. It's like we are asking them to start off in life with one hand tied behind their backs.

As a society we have taken some wrong turns, like replacing the grammar schools that did such a good job at helping people like me to get a start in life with others that have not had the same success rate. In the process of becoming more affluent and of having more of what we thought we wanted, we have actually become less community minded. We all have less time for one another and more possessions that we are fearful of losing. The less trusting we have become the more we have filled the world with CCTV cameras, all of us watching one another all the time. George Orwell was right about so many things when he wrote *1984*: he just predicted it all happening twenty-five years early.

In so many ways we now have the world we wished for and created for ourselves, but now we have it I am not so sure that it is better than what came before. This is the life that my family dreamed of when they came to England from various troubled parts of Europe, and the society that their generation fought for in the Second World War. In my early days as an impresario I would have loved to have been given the media opportunities that Andrew Lloyd Webber and Simon Cowell have exploited so successfully.

But in many other fundamental ways, nothing much has changed. For all the revolutions and innovations of the last half century the biggest selling records are still tracks like Englebert's 'Release Me', Slim Whitman's 'Rose Marie' and Bryan Adams' 'Everything I Do'. It seems that no matter how much technology might have changed the method of delivery since I set up a sound system at Romano's in Gerrard Street, and later in my offices at Chandos Place, people still like pretty much the same stuff they always have, and the huge success of the O2 Centre in London, and others like it around the world, shows the public still want to see their favourite artists playing live in much the same way as they did when they flocked to the music halls and later to The Beatles' concerts and my festivals at Wembley. Speaking of Wembley, I went to the venue very recently, as they want me to put the festival on again. I am seriously thinking about it.

★Acknowledgements★

There are so many people that I need to thank, not just for their help in producing this book, but for the kindness, support and understanding they have shown to me throughout my professional life – even when I was giving some of them a hard time. I would like to have told stories about everyone I have ever worked with but there just wasn't enough room in one book. I have tried to list as many as possible here, but apologies to anyone who feels they have been left out. It's nothing personal.

For the creation of this book, I would like to thank Andrew Crofts for helping me put some shape into a long life and Stuart Wheatman at Tonto Books who believed in my story enough to take it on. I would also like to thank Carmel Mannion for all her efforts to bring the resulting book to the attention of the world and Elliot Thomson for a wonderful cover design.

From the bottom of my heart I would like to thank my children for bringing me so much joy, both through their own lives and through the lives of the grandchildren they have given me.

Mervyn Conn
September 2010

A–Z of Artists And Shows

A
AG & Kate
Aine
Alan Price
Alan Sunderland
Albert Lee
Aladdin (pantomime)
Allon Young
Alvin Stardust
Anita Carter
Anne Murray
Anne Shelton
Annie (musical)
Anthony Newley
Arie den Dulk
Art Woods
Asleep At The Wheel
Astrud Gilberto

B
Barbara Fairchild
Barbara Mandrell
Barbara Windsor
Barbi Benton
The Barron Knights
Barry McCloud & The
 Bounty Hunters
The Basil Brush Show
Basil Hendricks
The Batchelors
The Beatles

Becky Hobbs
The Bellamy Brothers
Benny Goodman
Bernard Delfont
The Beverley Sisters
Big Guitars From Memphis
Bill Anderson
Bill Conlon
Bill Kenwright
Bill Maynard
Bill Monroe
Billy J Kramer
Billie Jo Spears
Billy Armstrong
Billy Burgoyne
Billy Condon
Billy Eckstine
Billy Joe Shaver
Billy Swan
Billy Walker
BJ Thomas
Blossom Dearie
Bo Diddley
Bob Brolly & Calvary
Bob Condon
Bob Harris
Bob Newman
Bob Young & The Double M
 Band
Bobby Bare
Bolshoi Ballet
Bolshoi Opera Company
Bonnie Dobson
Boxcar Willie
Boytorian
The Brazos Valley Boys
Brenda Lee
Brendan Quinn
Brian Chalker
Brian Coll
Brian Poole & The Tremeloes
The Big Line Dance (3,500:

Guinness Book Of Records)
The British Line Dancing
   Championships
The British Line Dancing
   Display Team
Brook Benton
Buck Owens
Buddy Emmons
Buddy Greco
Buffy Sainte-Marie
The Flying Burrito Brothers
The Byrds
Byron Whitman

C

Canones y Mantequilla
Carey Duncan
The Cates Sisters
Carl Jackson
Carl Perkins
Carl Smith
Carlene Carter
Carmen McRae
Carol Gordon
Carroll Baker
Caroline Hall
The Cass Family
The Carter Family
Cecil Gee
Charley Pride
Charlie Landsborough
Charlie Louvin
Charlie McCoy
Charlie Rich
Charlie Walker
The Cheap Seats
Chet Atkins
Chubby Checker
Chuck Berry
Chuck Glaser
Cilla Black
Cinderella (pantomime)

Cliff Bennett
Clodagh Rogers
Colin Crompton
Colleen Peterson
Colorado
Commander Cody & His Lost
   Planet Airmen
Connie Smith
The Conquerors
Conway Twitty
The Cotton Mill Boys
The Country Blue Boys
Country Fever
The Country Folk
Country Gazette
Cowboys New Grass Revival
Chris Farlow
Crispian St Peters
Crystal Gayle
Cynthia Clawson
Czech Country Beat

D

Dan Riley
Dana
Daniel O'Donnell
Danny Sheerin
Dave Barnes
Dave Berry & The Cruisers
Dave Bryant & Moonshine
Dave Clark Five
Dave Dee, Dozy, Beaky,
   Mick & Tich
Dave Sheriff
Dave & Sugar
David Allan
David Allan Coe
David Frizzell
Sir David Frost
David Jacobs
David Houston
The Dean Brothers

Declan Nerney
Del Reeves
Dermot Hegarty
Dennis Weaver
Derek Jacobi
Des O'Connor
Desi Egan
Diane Pfeifer
Diana Trask
Dick Damron
Dick Gregory
The Dillards
Dolly Parton
Doc Watson
Don Arden
Don Black
Don Everly
Don Gibson
Don Williams
Donna Fargo
Donovan
Dorothy Squires
Dottie West
Dottsy
Doug Kershaw
The Drifting Cowboys

E
Earl Scruggs
Earl Thomas Conley
Eartha Kitt
Ed Bruce
Ed Wooden
Eddie Calvert
Eddie Eastman
Eddie Mitchell
Edwin Hawkin
Elkie Brooks
Elvis Costello
ELO
Emerald
Emmylou Harris & The Hot

Band
Englebert Humperdinck
Eric Clapton
Ernest Tubb
Everly Brothers
Exile

F
Faron Young
Ferlin Huskey
Floyd Cramer
Fonograph
Footloose
Forrester Sisters
Foster & Allen
Frank Berry
Frank Ifield
The Frank Jennings Syndicate
Frank Yonco
Frankie McBride
Freda Payne
Freddie Davies
Freddie & The Dreamers
Freddie Fender
Freddie Hart
Free Spirit
Frisco

G
Gail Davis
Gene Watson
Gregg Turner
George Graham
George Hug & West Coast
George Jones
George Shearing
George Sewell
Georgette Jones
The Georgian State Dance
   Company
Georgie Fame & The Blue

207

Flames
George Hamilton lV
George Hamilton V
Gerry Ford
Glen Campbell
Gloria
Glory-Anne Carriere
The Gonks
Graham Fenton's Matchbox
Graham McHugh
Grandpa Jones
The Grumbleweeds
Guy Clark
Guy Mitchell

H

Hank Locklin
Hank Snow
Hank Thompson
The Hank Wangford Band
Hank Williams Jnr
Harry Secombe
Harvey Goldsmith
Hayden Thompson
Helen Carter
Herman's Hermits
The Hillsiders
Hogan's Heroes
The Hollies
Hoyt Axton
HS Krush
Hughie Green

I

Ian & Andy
Isla Grant

J

Jack & The Beanstalk
  (pantomime)
Jack Greene
James Royal

Jan Howard
Jana Jay
Jane Seymour
Janie Fricke
Jean Shepard
Jeannie Denver
Jeannie Pruett
Jeannie C Riley
Jeannie Seely
Jeff Hanna
Jerry Douglas
Jerry Foster
Jerry Jeff Walker
Jerry Lee Lewis
Jerry Mulligan
Jerry Stevens
Jess Conrad
Jessi Colter
Jessie Kent
Jim Aitken
Jim Glaser
Jim & Jesse McReynolds
Jim Ed Brown
Jimmy C Newman
Jimmy Payne
Jimmy Savile
Jimmy Tarbuck
Joan Regan
Jodi Miller
Jodle Birge
Joe Brown & The Bruvvers
Joe Collins
Joe Dolan
Joe Ely
Joe Loss Orchestra
Joe Stampley
Joe Sun
Joe William
John Carter Cash
John Hartford
John D Loudermilk
John Lynam

John McEuen
John McFall
John Wesley Ryles
John Ryan
John Schneider (*Dukes Of Hazzard*)
John Staunton
John Worthy
Johnny Carver
Johnny Cash
The Johnny Cash Show
Johnny Duncan
Johnny Gimble
Johnny Lee
Johnny Paycheck
Johnny Russell
Johnny Two Step
Johnny Wright
Jon Derek & Country Fever
The Johnny Young 4
The Jordanaires
Jose Feliciano
Judy Lindsey
Julie Rogers
June Carter Cash

K
Kathy Barnes
Kathy Durkin
Kathy Kay
Katie Moffatt
Kay Starr
Kaye Sisters
Keith Manifold
Keith Whitley
Kelly Foxton
Kelvin Henderson
Ken Dodd
Ken & Billie Ford
Ken Fryer
The Kendalls
Kenneth McKellar

Kenny Lynch
Kenny Rogers
Kenny Seratt
Kevin Sheerin
Kimmie Rhodes
Kitty Wells
Kris Kristofferson

L
Lacy J Dalton
Lance Percival
Lanie Smallwood
Larry Boone
Larry Cunningham
Larry Gatlin
Larry Grayson
Lateshift
Laura Conn
Lee Conway
Lee Moran
Lefty Frizzell
The Legarde Twins
Leo Sayer
Leon Everette
Leslie Crowther
Les Dennis
Lew Grade
Linda Cassady
Lindisfarne
Little Ginny
Little Jimmy Dickens
Lloyd Green
Logue & McCool
London Symphony Orchestra
Lonnie Donegan
Loretta Lynn
Lorrie Morgan
Lou Bellison
Lou Christie
Louise Morrissey
Lulu
Lynch & Dawson

Lynn Anderson

M

Mac Wiseman
Magna Carta
Malcolm MacDonald
Mamas & Papas
Manfred Mann
Margo Smith
Marie Osmond
Mark Gray
Mark O'Connor
Marlene Dietrich
Marmalade
Martha Reeves & The
  Vandellas
Marty Robbins
Marty Wilde
Marvin Rainwater
Mary Bailey
Mary Chapin Carpenter
Mary Duff
Mary Lou Turner
Matt Leavy
Matt Monro
Max Bygraves
Max Perry
Medicine Bow
Mel McDaniel
Mel Tillis
Mel Torme
Melba Montgomery
Memphis Roots
The Mercy Brothers
Merle Haggard
Merle Kilgore
Merle Watson
Merrill Moore
Michael Black
Michael Commins
Michael Doucet
Michael (Lord) Levy

Michael O'Brien
Mick Clerkin
Mick Flavin
Mick Lube
Mickey Newbury
Micky Duff
Micky Gilley
The Mighty Avons
Mike & Bernie Winters
Mike Yarwood
Miki & Griff
The Mintings
Molly Bee
Moe Bandy
The Moody Blues
The Moody Brothers
Murray Kash

N

Nada Urbankova & Country
  Beat
Nancy Wilson
Narvel Felts
The Nashville Superpickers
Nashville Teens
Nat Stuckey
The New Seekers
The New Strangers
Newgrass Revival
Nick Lowe
Nina & Frederick
Nina Simone
The Nitty Gritty Dirt Band
NJ Big Band
Noel Andrews
Norman Wisdom

O

The Oakridge Boys
The O'Kanes
Olivia Newton John
Orange Blossom Sound

The Osmond Brothers (Alan,
  Wayne, Merrill, Jay)
Ozark Mountain Daredevils

P

Paschal Mooney
Pat Campbell
Pat Jennings
Patrice
Patrick Duffy (*Dallas*)
The Patsy Cline Story
  (musical)
Patsy Powell
Patty Lovelace
Paul Kennerley
Paul McCartney
Paul Richey
The Peddlers
Peggie Lee
Peggy Sue
Perry Groves
Pete Brady
Peter Noone
Peter Rowan
Peter Walker
Peters & Lee
Petula Clark
Phil Brady & The Ranchers
Phil Solomon
Philomena Begley
Pinkertons Colours
Pinto Bennett
Poacher
PJ Proby
Porter Wagoner
The Pretty Things
Procol Harem
Puss In Boots (pantomime)

R

Ralph Emery
Ralph Murphy

Ramsey Lewis
Randy VanWarmer
Rankarna & Mats Radberg
Rattlesnake Annie
Ray Allen
Ray Cameron
Ray Lynam & The Hillbillies
Ray Pillow
Ray Stevens
Razzie Bailey
Raymond Froggatt
Razzie Bailey
Red Sovine
The Red Army Ensemble
Reg Varney
Rex Allen Jnr
Rita Coolidge
Rob Fowler
Roberta Flack
The Rockin' Berries
Rod McKuen
Rodeo Ruth
Rodney Crowell
Roger Whittaker
Rolf Harris
The Rolling Stones
Roly Daniels
Ronnie Corbett
Ronnie Kennedy
Ronnie Milsap
Ronnie Prophet
Ronnie Robins
Ronnie Scott
Ronnie Wood
Rose-Marie
Roseanne Cash
Rosemary Clooney
Rosie Flores
Roxon Roadshow
Roy Acuff
Roy Clark
Roy Drusky

Roy Orbison
Roy Wood
Royal Philharmonic Orchestra
Royal Scots Guards

S
Sally O'Brien
Sammy Davis Jr
Sandy Kelly
The Sarah Jory Band
Sarah Vaughan
Saskie & Serge
Scarlett Conn
Scooter Lee
Scot McKenzie
Sharon Haynes
Shelly West
Shoji Tabuchi
Skeeter Davies
Sleepy LaBeef
Slim Whitman
Small Faces
Sonny Wright
The Sorrows
Spencer Davis
Spike Milligan
The Spinners
Springfield Revival
Stan Getz
Stan Laundon
Station Break
The Statler Brothers
Stella Parton
Stephane Grappelli
Stephanie Lawrence
Steps (pop band)
Steve Cosby
The Stoneman Family
Stonewall Jackson
The Strauss Tour
Stu Phillips
Stubby Kaye

Susan McCann
Susan Maughan
Suzanne Prentice
Suzie Allanson
Suzy Bogguss
Syd & Eddie Little
Syd Lawrence Orchestra
Sydney Devine
T
Tammy Cline
Tammy Wynette
The Tammy Wynette Story
   (musical)
Tanya Tucker
Tapping Harlem (musical)
Ted Heath & His Orchestra
Ted Rodgers
Teddy Nelson
Teddy Wilson
Temptations
Tender Mercies
The Tennessee Mountain
   Boys
Terry Gibbs
Terry Hollowell
Terry McKenna
Terry McMillan
Terry Neill
Terry Stafford
Tex Ritter
Tex Withers
Them
Three Steps To Heaven
   (musical)
Timi Yuro
Tokyo Matsu
Tom Allen
Tom Gilmore
Tom Gribbin & The Saltwater
   Cowboys
Tom Jennings
Tom Jones

212

Tom T Hall
Tommy Collins
Tommy Overstreet
Tommy Steele
Tompall & The Glaser
Brothers
Tony Byworth
Tony Goodacre
Tony Griffin & Blueberry
Buckle
Tony Hatch
Tony Hiller
Tony Loughman
Tony Murray
The Tony Rouse Band
Townes Van Zandt
The Troggs
The Tumbleweeds
TR Dallas
Twinkle
Two's Company

U
The Ukrainian Dance
Company
Unit 4 + 2
The United

V
Van Morrison
Vern Gosdin
Vernon Oxford
Vic Groves
Vince Hill
Vince Power
The Virginia Boys
The Virginians

W
The Walker Brothers
Wally Whyton
Wanda Jackson

Waylon Jennings
Wayne Fontana & The
Mindbenders
The Wedgewoods
Wendel Adkins
Wendy Holcombe
Wes Buchanan
Wesley Orbison
Wesley Parker
West Coast
The Who
The Wilburn Brothers
Willard Pearce
Willie Nelson
Wizzard
Woody Herman Orchestra

Y
The Yardbirds
Yootha Joyce